DATE DUE			

D1122959

CULTURES OF THE WORLD

THAILAND

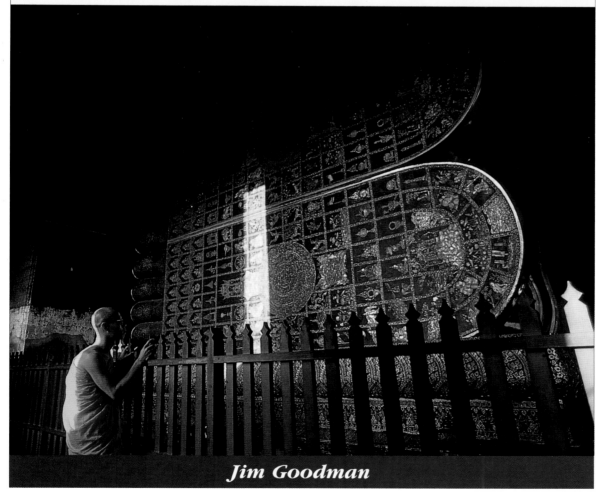

Jim Goodman

MARSHALL CAVENDISH
New York • London • Sydney

Reference edition reprinted 2000 by
Marshall Cavendish Corporation
99 White Plains Road
Tarrytown
New York 10591

© Times Media Private Limited 1994, 1991

Originated and designed by
Times Books International, an imprint of
Times Media Private Limited, a member of the
Times Publishing Group

Printed in Singapore

Library of Congress Cataloging-in-Publication Data:
Goodman, Jim.
    Thailand / James Edward Goodman.—
    Reference ed.
      p. cm.—(Cultures of the world)
    Includes bibliographical references and index.
    Summary: Explores in text and photographs the
intricate and often exotic history, as well as the current
realities, of this dynamic Southeast Asian kingdom.
      ISBN 1-85435-402-7
      1. Thailand—Juvenile literature [1. Thailand.]
I. Title. II. Series.
DS563.5.G66 1991
959.3—dc20   91-17719
                          CIP
                          AC

INTRODUCTION

THAILAND HAS long had a reputation as an exotic and mysterious tropical wonderland ever since its first ambassadors reached the court of the French king, Louis XIV. That image was reinforced by Hollywood, along with the reports of soldiers and sailors who found it ideal for rest and recreation.

Thailand is known by many names—the Land of Elephants, the Land of Smiles, the Land of Enchantment. Its charm and easygoing lifestyle, its beautiful beaches and resorts have attracted a great number of visitors every year. Few who come are aware of what it offers, much less its interesting culture or its long and complex history—one of Asia's oldest and most colorful.

As part of the series *Cultures of the World*, this book looks beyond the tourist brochures to examine Thailand and its people.

CONTENTS

One of Thailand's many miniature shrines.

3 INTRODUCTION

7 GEOGRAPHY
Climate • Creation • Mixed network • Mae Nam Chao Phraya Basin • Northern hills • Isan • Peninsular Thailand • Flora and fauna

19 HISTORY
First settlers • Mons, Khmers, and Indian influence • Early Thai kingdoms • Ayutthaya • The Chakri kings • Democracy

29 GOVERNMENT
Provinces • Villages • Upholding the law • The army

35 ECONOMY
Toward a modern economy • Out on the farms • Tourism • Vanishing occupations • The decline of the elephant

41 THAIS
Tais • Demography • Sino-Thais and Thai Moslems • People of the Isan • Traditional costumes • Hill tribes • Individual tribes

51 LIFESTYLE
Thai society • Thai way • The smile • Family • Births • Growing up • Marriage • Career • Free time • Deaths • Thai houses

67 RELIGION
Pre-Buddhism • Buddhist practices • Other religions • Fortune telling • Thai astrology • Mind and body therapy • Amulets

CONTENTS

77 LANGUAGE
*Thai and its dialects • The Thai alphabet • Meaning in Thai names
• Body language*

85 ART
*Literary kings • Buddhist architecture • Performing arts • Other
theatrical arts • Hill tribal music • Weaving • Embroidery
• Akha jackets • Sculpture and painting • Handicrafts*

99 LEISURE
Animal combats • Games • Exercise • Recreation • Entertainment

107 FESTIVALS
*Traditional Thai festivals • Chinese festivals • Other festivals
• Tribal festivals • Making new festivals • Beauty contests*

117 FOOD
A trditional meal • Rice • Regional tastes • Tribal food

122 MAP

124 QUICK NOTES

125 GLOSSARY

126 BIBLIOGRAPHY AND INDEX

**Dolls made by one of
the hill tribes of
Thailand.**

GEOGRAPHY

THE KINGDOM OF THAILAND lies at the southern part of the continent of Asia, in the heart of Southeast Asia. With an area of 198,456 square miles, it is slightly smaller than France and stretches between 5° and 21° north latitude. From its northernmost town of Mae Sai to its southern border, it is 930 miles long, while its width at its greatest is 500 miles. To the east and northeast, it shares borders with Kampuchea and Laos; to the northwest and west is Myanmar (formerly Burma). To the southeast is the Gulf of Thailand; its western peninsular provinces overlook the Andaman Sea, and the south is bounded by Malaysia.

CLIMATE

Thailand's climate is subject to annual monsoons. In the hot, dry months of summer, the fierce tropical heat draws in moist and humid air from the south seas. This collects until it falls as seasonal rain over the region. As summer passes, the process reverses. Cold, dry winds from central Asia blow south and usher in a cool, dry season. This cycle then repeats itself.

The climate in Thailand is subject to unchanging heat and high humidity; it is hot nearly all year long, with heavy rains from May through October.

Opposite: **The calm, clear waters off Ko Phi Phi, one of Thailand's favorite resort islands near Phuket off the Andaman Sea. It was near this place that the James Bond movie,** *The Man with the Golden Gun*, **was filmed.**

Below: **Two men in a boat with the ruins of the legendary old city of Sukhothai in the background. The Thai people look upon Sukhothai and its king, Ramkhamhaeng, the way Westerners regard Camelot and King Arthur.**

The beautiful Mae Sa waterfalls near Chiang Mai is a popular attraction for both tourists and local residents.

CREATION

Some scientists believe that the land that is now Thailand began to take shape 60 million years ago, when volcanoes to the south pushed the Indonesian island of Sumatra up against the Malay Peninsula, producing southern Thailand. About 35 million years later, what is now India crashed into Asia, creating the mighty Himalaya Mountains and causing smaller ranges, such as those that are found on Thailand's western borders to emerge.

Rising water later filled some areas around Southeast Asia, forming the present-day Gulf of Thailand, a shallow sea less than 230 feet deep to the south of Thailand. It also gave the Malay Peninsula, the Indonesian islands and Thailand their current shapes.

Thailand's contours are still subject to change. The mountains are young and there are occasional earthquakes. During the monsoon season, rainfall is both heavy and quick, saturating the water in the hills. This forms a wet surface where the topsoil can suddenly give way; this is why there are many avalanches and landslides in the region.

Thailand's many rivers swell with the rains, carrying off mud and clay and depositing it elsewhere around the country's plains. Bangkok, which in ancient times lay beside the sea, is now 25 miles from the coast, but its low altitude places it only a few feet above the highest tides, which can sometimes roll inland as far as 19 miles from the shore.

A pony pulling a cart is a common sight in southern Thailand.

MIXED NETWORK

Ancient Thai settlements were situated on rivers that provided avenues for transportation and communication. Eventually people connected these rivers by means of canals, which now crisscross the heavily-populated river basins.

Boats of all kinds were the first means used to bring goods and produce to the markets and towns. Despite Thailand's recent construction of new, modern roads throughout the country, canals and rivers still play an important part in the transportation of people and goods.

Thailand opened its first railway service in Bangkok in 1896 and by 1910 had completed the tracks to Nakhon Ratchasima, the nearest major town in the northeast. Railway and road construction, especially since World War II, have been effective in bringing administrative services and economic progress to the provinces.

Today, the country is experiencing a boom in roads and automobiles. Even the most remote areas, once only accessible by foot, can now be reached by roads.

One of Bangkok's many temples beside the Chao Phraya River. This is the main river of the Menam Chao Basin, or Central Plains. To the Thais, it is the equivalent of Egypt's Nile. Although less than 200 miles long, the Chao Phraya is one of the most important means of connecting Bangkok to the rest of the Plains.

MAE NAM CHAO PHRAYA BASIN

The Mae Nam Chao Phraya Basin, also known as the Central Plains, is the country's most important rice-producing region as well as its most industrialized area. It is fertile and contains one-third of Thailand's population. At Nakhon Sawan, three rivers from the north join to form the Chao Phraya River, which flows through the heart of Thailand, passing Bangkok en route to the sea. This network of rivers forms the basin.

Bangkok, with nearly six million people, is the nation's political, commercial, and financial capital. It is 40 times larger than Chiang Mai, Thailand's second largest city. It is also a major industrial center, with over 30,000 workshops and factories. Though it suffers from problems typical of any fast-growing city—pollution, traffic, crime, and overcrowding—it continues to lure people from all parts of the country.

The Mae Nam Chao Phraya Basin is also the site of several historical towns, including Ayutthaya the former capital; Lop Buri; and Nakhon Pathom. To the east lie the coastal areas and mineral-rich Chanthaburi; to the west lies Kanchanaburi, the most remote part of the country.

FLOATING MARKETS

A bit of Old Thailand survives just north of Bangkok at Klong Damnoen Saduak. It is popularly known as the Floating Market.

Klong ("klohng") means "canal" and there are 83 in metropolitan Bangkok alone. Along these canals, there are usually over 10,000 boats carrying all sorts of vegetables, fruits, dried fish, rice, flowers, and other produce; others are miniature floating kitchens where they sell ready-to-eat food like noodles, fried bananas, fresh coconut milk, and desserts wrapped in banana leaves.

The vendors, usually dressed in dark blue clothes and straw hats to ward off the sunlight, load their boats with produce early each morning and paddle to the *klong* to form the market, where all buying and selling takes place on the water.

A generation ago, such vendors used to load up at 2 a.m. and attach small oil lamps to their masts as signals to other boats. Hundreds of these twinkling lights assembled at the main market *klong* awaiting the dawn presented a breathtaking sight. Today, the floating market still presents a colorful and exotic side of modern Thailand, although there is criticism over its growing commercialization.

Bangkok is called the "Venice of the East" because of its many canals or "klong." In the morning, the "klong" is filled with all sorts of boats. There is only one rule—the middle of the "klong" is usually left open for passing. That is until it, too, gets clogged up. Then a special traffic policeman on his boat comes along and tries his best to untangle the mess.

NORTHERN HILLS

The green, rolling hills of Thailand's northernmost provinces are actually part of the great Himalayas, although they only average 3,300–6,600 feet.

The Ping, Wang, Yom, Nan, and Pa Sak rivers flow between the ranges, eventually coming together to form the Chao Phraya River. This region is filled with beautiful scenery, waterfalls, and caves. It also has the greatest extremes in climate. Although the nights after the monsoon season are often chilly, the daytime temperature in April or May often hits 104°F.

In the past, thick forests covered most of the land, but slash-and-burn agriculture, population pressures, and extensive commercial logging have critically reduced the forests, that were once filled with teak and other hardwood trees.

The area is also rich in history and culture. Some of the earliest Thai kingdoms originated here, in towns like Chiang Saen, Chiang Rai, Chiang Mai, Phayao, and Nan.

Ancient influences are evident in local architecture, and the hills are home to colorful tribal peoples with a way of life very different from that of the Central Plains dwellers.

One of the many waterfalls in the northern hills of Thailand. Most of these places are known only to Thais, who come from all parts of the country to swim and relax.

THE GOLDEN TRIANGLE

Where the Mae Sai and Mekong rivers meet also marks the point where Thailand, Laos, and Myanmar come together. Known as the Golden Triangle, the area has a long and infamous reputation as a leading center in opium and heroin production.

While Thailand has destroyed most of its poppy fields and persuaded farmers to grow other crops, the fight is far from over. Many other poppy fields are in the remote and war-torn provinces across the rivers, making the job extremely difficult.

ISAN

Thailand's northeastern provinces, known as the Isan, lie on a flat limestone plateau that is bounded by the low but steep Phetchabun Range to the west, the Dongrak Range along the Kampuchean border to the south, and the Mekong River to the east.

Poor soil and little irrigation characterize the region, which lies in a "rain shadow"—an area that has little rain. Unlike the Central Plains, where farms are everywhere, many parts of the Isan cannot be successfully cultivated.

Still, there are "holes" in the "rain shadow," where the amount of rainfall produces seasonal swamps in some places but fertile patches of land elsewhere. On these patches, the soil is good for cultivation.

To the east of the Isan lies the Mekong River. From its source in the Tibetan Plateau in China, the Mekong flows 2,817 miles to meet the sea in southern Vietnam. Flowing through the southwestern Chinese province of Yunnan, the Mekong separates Myanmar from Laos immediately north of Thailand and then forms the boundary between Thailand and Laos for 1,000 miles—nearly the entire length of the Thai-Laotian border.

With the gradual reopening of Laos to trade and tourism, the Mekong— for years commercially quiet—is becoming busier. This is very good news for the long-neglected economy of the Isan.

What do mulberry trees of the poor region of the Isan have to do with the rich people of New York and Paris? The mulberry trees are grown by the hundreds to feed worms. These worms in turn spin the silks that are sent to the largest cities in the United States and France to make expensive clothing.

An aerial view of the strange but breathtaking Phangnga Bay near Phuket.

PENINSULAR THAILAND

South of the Mae Nam Chao Phraya Basin, the upper part of the long Malay Peninsula is divided between Myanmar and Thailand by the Bilauktaung Mountain Range. Along this narrow strip from the Andaman Sea down to the Malaysian border, both coastlines belong to Thailand.

The limestone and crystalline mountains that continue down the peninsula—some rising up to 5,000 feet—are often of unusual shapes. Beautiful islands lie off either side of the peninsula, sites of some of Asia's best beaches. Bays on the west coast often feature resorts, villages on stilts in the sea, and colorful coral reefs.

The climate in the south is less extreme than in other parts of the nation, for the peninsula receives in some places up to 240 inches of rainfall every year, three times that of Bangkok.

The western side of the region, next to the deep Andaman Sea, is home to countless plantations growing rubber and palm oil trees. Tin deposits also lie in valleys and off the coast. The area along the Gulf of Thailand is devoted mostly to rice farming.

Except for Hat Yai, a commercial and transportation town just north of the Malaysian border, the south's most important towns are all along the coasts: from Pattani, Songkhla, Nakhon Si Thammarat, and Surat Thani on the Gulf side to Ranong, Phuket, and Krabi on the Andaman side. Thick tropical forests cover the mountains of the peninsula.

FLORA AND FAUNA

Thailand's location in the monsoon area of the world once assured it of heavy rainforests and abundant animal life. Unfortunately, civilization has reduced much of these natural assets.

FLORA Thailand still boasts extensive wooded areas, with valuable trees like teak, rosewood, ebony, and—in the south—oil palm and rubber. Evergreens, sappanwood, and casuarina are found throughout the country, while mangrove swamps occupy some deltas and coastlines of the south. Thailand is filled with flowering shrubs, trees, and plants. Among the most common and famous is the lotus, which is rooted in ponds but flowers above the water surface. This feature has attracted poets and the abundant lotus is a religious symbol to many.

The lotus, the favorite flower in Thailand, is found almost everywhere in the country, either the real thing or as a design motif. For Buddhists, it is a symbol of purity and perfection.

Another is the orchid, which grows both in jungles and special nurseries, particularly in the north. There is also the jasmine, a favorite offering at temples; and the frangipani, the bougainvillea, and the hibiscus. In the rain-soaked peninsular jungles, you can find carnivorous plants like the insect-eating pitcher plant, and some that rely on other trees or plants to live, like the epiphytes, rattan, and other vines and creepers.

A complete list of native vegetation includes plants and trees that bear bananas, durians, oranges, mangoes, papayas, and jackfruits, among others.

FAUNA The different species of wildlife, as well as their numbers, are difficult to observe in Thailand's rainforests, national parks, and game reserves. Unlike Africa or North America, most of these animals stay in dark, dense jungles.

The largest mammals living in these areas include the tiger, leopard, gaur, deer of various sizes, tapir, boar, civet, wildcat, porcupine, monkey, flying squirrel, and wild elephant.

Pheasants are the most common bird species. Eagles and parakeets are less common, while songbirds and blue-tailed gibbons are rare. Nevertheless, the jungles house a great range of insect- or fruit- and seed-eating species. They also have a large variety of insects, including armored beetles and moths with wingspans of 12 inches or more. Scorpions and spiders prowl the secluded areas as well, especially when it is raining.

Reptiles and amphibians thrive in Thailand's

Thailand has many varieties of beautiful and exotic flowers.

tropical climate. The most dangerous are snakes like the cobra, the krait and different kinds of vipers, and the crocodiles that live in rivers near the sea. Pythons, other harmless snakes, and lizards of all sizes also reside in these areas.

Thailand's surrounding seas hold thousands of species of fish, plus other marine life like the crabs, lobsters, cockles, clams, and mussels that find their way to Thai dinner tables. Along the west coast are fantastic stretches of undersea corals, although tourist development presents a new threat to these fragile and delicate sea creatures.

THE LAST FRONTIER

Kanchanaburi is Thailand's least-populated province, in spite of being full of lush jungles and thick forests, scenic rivers and the country's most beautiful waterfalls.

Also in the region stands a strange-looking bridge across the Meklang River. Nothing special about it, until you learn that the Meklang is also known as the Kwai Yai, one of the most infamous names of World War II. During the war, Japanese soldiers forced thousands of Allied prisoners of war to construct the "Bridge on the River Kwai." In the process, an estimated 116,000 native laborers and prisoners of war died because of beatings, starvation, diseases, and exhaustion. Nearby, war graves mark the remains of nearly 7,000 Allied soldiers. The event was commemorated in the powerful 1957 movie of the same name.

Nowadays the province has few visitors, mainly because of the presence of disease-carrying mosquitoes. Strangely, these mosquitoes have played an important role in preserving Kanchanaburi. The threat of brain fever and death resulting from mosquito bites discourages many people from going there.

During the dry season hundreds of bonfires are lit in the countryside, and Thais rake and sweep the rubbish and fallen leaves from around every house. Are they preparing for an outdoor party? No, they are instead looking for snakes! The area around the house is swept clean and the burning grass attracts snakes. The people will capture as many snakes as possible and sell them to the Snake Farm. Poisonous snakes fetch the most money; harmless snakes fetch less; and little snakes are fed to the big ones! At the present rate, Thailand will some day be a snake-free kingdom.

HISTORY

LITTLE IS KNOWN OF THAILAND'S prehistory. The available evidence is so scant that not much can be assumed either. Some scientists believe that parts of Thailand were first settled in the Stone Age; skeletons dating from then have been discovered in Kanchanaburi Province. Mysterious rock paintings were found in cliffs near the Thai-Laotian-Kampuchean border as well as at Ko Kian in Phang Nga. But aside from estimating that they are at least 3,000 years old, scientists know next to nothing of the artists.

Opposite: **This Khmer sculpture indicates Hindu influences.**

FIRST SETTLERS

The first genuine settlements—where people lived in groups, practiced agriculture, made pottery, and wove cloth—were on hillsides. By 2000 B.C., there were several throughout the country. The most important were two in the extreme northeast—at Non Nok Tha and Ban Chiang. It is generally accepted that the Ban Chiang settlement was started around 3500 B.C. By 1000 B.C., it was a complex culture that also produced outstanding ceramics. In its last period, from 300 B.C. to A.D. 300, it achieved a high degree of craftsmanship in painted pottery, bronze and iron tools, and bronze and glass jewelry. Much of this was discovered when burial sites were dug up, for the citizens of Ban Chiang buried their dead along with large amounts of goods.

Above: **The ruins of the Wat Raj Burana in the ancient city of Ayutthaya.**

MONS, KHMERS, AND INDIAN INFLUENCE

The first Indian immigrants to the Malay Peninsula began arriving in the 3rd century B.C. Around the birth of Christ, they had established, according to Chinese records of the time, 10 city-states—the most important being Nakhon Si Thammarat.

When the Mons, a people originally from southern China, migrated to the Mae Nam Chao Phraya Basin, they took over civilized areas as well as Indian ideas of religion and handicraft. They also established the kingdom of Dvaravati at Nakhon Pathom in the sixth century. Later, they expanded north to Haripunjaya (now Lamphun), south into the Malay Peninsula, and west into Burma, where they founded an important state at Pegu.

The Khmers, who were relatives of the Mons, settled in the Lower Mekong and expanded east. In a ninth century war, they overpowered the Mons in the Central Plains. Like the Mons, the Khmers adopted Indian customs and laws. The king's authority was identified by sacred powers and displayed during public ceremonies.

Khmer power peaked in the 11th century, until King Anawrahta of Burma pushed them from his country and even briefly occupied the Central Plains. But the Khmers still controlled much of Thailand through outposts at Lop Buri and Phimai. They also controlled states in the south. But in the early 13th century, a revolt in the west signaled the rise of a new group that replaced the Khmers at the center of Thai history—the people of Sukhothai.

EARLY THAI KINGDOMS

Groups of Thais began migrating into present-day Thailand perhaps as early as the eighth century. The Khmers began employing them as soldiers

The spires and ruins of Sukhothai. It was in this great city that Thai architecture really developed. The architects of Sukhothai created buildings with great spires and multi-tiered rooftops. These patterns are still followed by today's builders.

in the 12th century. But as Mon and Khmer power decreased, other states began to rise.

In 1238, Thais at Sukhothai not only refused to pay the customary water tribute to their Khmer lords, they also threw them out of the land and established a new state. A new leader, Sri Indradit, took over the throne. He was more like a father than a king to his people; more like a respected chieftain than an absolute ruler.

Under its greatest king, Ramkhamhaeng (?1279–?1317), Sukhothai conquered Khmer territory as far south as Nakhon Si Thammarat. This same monarch also created the first Thai alphabet and introduced to his people an appreciation for the arts. His death in 1300 spelled the decline of the Sukhothai empire.

First, the provinces around Sukhothai broke off all ties to the empire. Then the Mons of Pegu attacked and captured part of the Malay Peninsula. Finally, a new state arose and, in 1378, attacked and conquered Sukhothai. From then on, the kingdom of Ayutthaya, founded only in 1350, was the mightiest of all Thai states.

A gateway to the ruins of Ayutthaya. Built on an island that was formed by the three rivers that meet there, Ayutthaya survived for 400 years and its beauty was reported even in Europe. At its zenith, during the 17th century, it was the largest city in southern Asia and had a population greater than that of London at that time.

AYUTTHAYA

Ayutthaya was a state where the king was lord over all life. A royal language was even used when speaking to or of him and his family. Ayutthayan society was organized under King Trailok (1448–88). Nobles of different grades were ranked and given titles according to how much land they had; commoners were not allowed to have ordinary relationships with them. Slavery was common, the victims usually prisoners of war.

Expansion and war with its neighbors characterized Ayutthaya's first two centuries. Having eliminated Sukhothai, the kingdom of Ayutthaya, also known as Siam, began conquering the south.

In 1431, King Boromaraja II sacked the Khmer city of Angkor Thom, forcing the Khmers to move to Phnom Penh. This put an end to the Khmer's power in the region. But Siam was not as successful against the northern kingdom of Chiang Mai. Under the reign of King Tilokaraja, Chiang Mai withstood all of Siam's attacks.

Meanwhile a new threat emerged on Siam's western flank when ambitious Burmese kings began marching into the land. Even Chiang Mai

A GREEK IN THE COURT OF SIAM

Among the many adventurers who journeyed across Asia in the 17th century, one of the most spectacular was a clever Greek sailor named Constantine Phaulkon—also known as the Falcon of Siam.

As an employee of the British East India Company, Phaulkon caught the eye of King Narai during trade negotiations. Quick at mastering the Thai language as well as the nuances of court behavior, Phaulkon soon became a special adviser to the king. Under Phaulkon's guidance, Siam profited a great deal from its foreign trade with the Europeans. Phaulkon's rise displeased his former employers, the British, so he switched his favors to the French.

Meanwhile, the court of France wanted Phaulkon to persuade the king to become a Catholic. The Falcon's efforts angered the Buddhist court so much that when Narai died, the next king immediately had Phaulkon beheaded and drove most of the Europeans out of the country.

fell to the invaders in 1557. Ayutthaya itself surrendered in 1569.

Siam became Burmese territory until 1584 when Prince Naresuan, taking advantage of a war in Burma, declared independence. Naresuan became king in 1590, and in three years, drove the Burmese completely out of the region. He became ruler of a vast region, including all of the land to the north and parts of Laos.

In the next century, Siam found itself involved with the West. Dutch merchants set up trade in the south at Pattani in 1601, and English traders came to Ayutthaya in 1612. European rivalry for trade and port privileges peaked under Narai the Great (1656–88). Siam sent ambassadors to France and the French king, Louis XIV, sent one to Narai in return.

But upon Narai's death, the Europeans suddenly found themselves out of favor, while rebellions broke out all over Siam. The Burmese immediately took the opportunity to occupy the north. A weakened Siam was now no match for the Burmese. While Ayutthaya enjoyed one last period of stability under Boromakot (1733–58), in April 1767 Burmese soldiers put the capital to flames.

"I stood…in admiration of the strong great city, seated upon an island round which flowed a river three times the size of the Seine. There rode ships from France, Britain, Holland, China and Japan, while innumerable boats and gilded barges rowed by 60 men plied to and fro…I do not know whether I have conveyed to you the impression of a beautiful view, but certainly I myself have never seen a lovelier."

—the Frenchman Abbé de Choisy, writing home about Ayutthaya.

When King Taskin was going mad, his Thai subjects called General Chao Phraya Chakri back from Laos in 1782. They then took Taskin off the throne and executed him by hitting him on the head with a sandalwood club, a method of death reserved only for royalty because it sheds no blood. Then they put Phraya Chakri on the throne and proclaimed him king, thus starting the dynasty that has ruled until the present.

THE CHAKRI KINGS

When Ayutthaya fell, a Siamese general named Taksin was in the area. Gathering followers, he retook the city later that year, but the destruction of Ayutthaya had been so thorough that he decided to move the capital farther downriver to Thonburi.

With the aid of two brother generals, Chao Phraya Chakri and Chao Phraya Surasih, Taksin subdued fierce vassals, beat off another Burmese attack, and captured the north. But success eventually drove him insane, and he became extremely cruel. His generals removed him from the throne and executed him in 1782.

Chao Phraya Chakri, better known as Rama I, became the new king. He began the Chakri dynasty that still exists today. Rama I moved the capital again, this time to Bangkok, constructing a city on the model of Ayutthaya. He also revived Thai art and literature, partly by calling upon the memories of the old people who had escaped Ayutthaya's destruction.

Europe at that time was preoccupied with the Napoleonic Wars. But from 1818, beginning with a Portuguese treaty, Siam once again opened contacts with the West. Generally aimed at obtaining favorable trading terms and privileges, treaties were established with Britain in 1826 and the United States in 1833.

Meanwhile, both Britain and France began conquering Siam's neighbors. At this critical point, Siam was blessed with the reigns of two outstanding rulers who were well versed in Western ways. They preserved the country's independence by setting up vital reforms that modernized and strengthened the nation.

The first was King Mongkut, or Rama IV (1851–68), a widely traveled ex-monk who built roads and hired foreign teachers. His successor, Chulalongkorn, ruled until 1910. Chulalongkorn eliminated submissive behavior in his presence, abolished slavery, improved national and local administration, and oversaw the development of railways, trams, automobiles, and the hiring of foreign advisers to serve in his government.

The next ruler, Rama VI (1910–25), entered Siam in the First World War on the Allied side. This led to treaty improvements with the United States and France.

Rama VI also introduced surnames and compulsory education, making Siam the first country in Asia to do so. Siam was now catching up with the developed world. However, a restless new social class was growing that considered the absolute monarchy a barrier to future progress.

Under Rama VII, Siam's political crisis peaked. The Great Depression of the 1930s hit rice exports especially hard, creating financial problems. The king tried to solve this with a new tax on salaries, but the move angered the people.

In 1932, a group of European educated army officers and intellectuals overthrew the government and announced the forming of a constitutional monarchy, thereby limiting the king's powers.

A painting of King Rama I, the founder of the present Chakri dynasty, at the royal palace.

DEMOCRACY

Besides announcing the beginning of a constitutional monarchy, the new rulers immediately extended elementary education, improved the administration of the nation, and changed the country's name from Siam to Thailand—which means "Land of the Free."

Under Marshal Pibun Songgram, who assumed power in 1938, Thailand demanded the return of territory in Laos and Kampuchea that formerly belonged to Siam. This attitude placed them in Japan's corner during World War II. The government declared war on the United States, but Thailand's ambassador in Washington refused to deliver the declaration, stating that it did not represent the people's will. The United States said it did not recognize the declaration anyway.

After the war, Thailand returned captured territory while the United States asked Britain and France to drop their other claims. This started a special relationship America has since enjoyed with Thailand.

Tragedy, however, marked the immediate post-war period when King Rama VIII was mysteriously assassinated in 1946. The government fell when the army, announcing it had assumed the role of "protector of the nation," staged a coup. Pibun Songgram returned to power for 10 years until another military coup ousted him.

The new government promoted investment. The effects of the Vietnam War also helped economic growth, while leading to a rising middle class that did not like the way the country was being ruled. So in October 1973, a student-led revolution took place. When the army refused to obey orders and the king indicated that he, too, favored a change, the government gave up. Thailand now moved more toward socialism. Many students supported farmer and labor movements. When the Communists became powerful in Indochina, Thailand's government requested that the United States close

The Royal Family of Thailand: King Bhumibol Adulyadej, Queen Sirikit, Prince Maha Vajiralongkorn, and Princess Maha Chakri Sirindhorn. The king and queen have another daughter, Princess Chulabhorn.

down its military bases in the country because they did not want any trouble with neighboring Vietnam.

Thailand's leadership crisis ended in 1980 when Prem Tinsulanonda took over. He governed for eight years, overseeing rapid development, peace, and the decline of socialism. Upon his retirement Thai politics entered an unstable period, with top military officers attempting to wield power against the wishes of a newly articulate middle class who desired greater democracy. This tension led to an eventual confrontation and crackdown in May, 1992, in which scores of Bangkok demonstrators were killed. In the aftermath new elections were held; the pro-military parties lost and a new coalition gained power under Prime Minister Chuan Leekpai.

The highly popular King Bhumibol (Rama IX) has remained monarch for the whole of this period. Beyond his ceremonial role, he frequently visits all parts of the country and sponsors many development programs for his people. The king is held in great esteem by his subjects. It was largely due to his personal intervention that the violent political crisis of 1992 was defused.

GOVERNMENT

THE 1978 CONSTITUTION states that the king is the head of the state and his sovereign power comes from the people. An addition to the Constitution promulgated on December 8, 1991, provides for a National Assembly of 270 appointed senators and 360 elected representatives, who must be at least 25 years old and serve a four-year term.

Real power belongs to the prime minister, whose office forms national policies and manages several financial and development offices. Constitutional amendments passed in the wake of the May, 1992 uprising require that the position be held only by an elected representative. The prime minister is also the chairman of the cabinet, which can have up to 44 ministers.

Laws may be proposed to the National Assembly either by the members of the assembly or the cabinet of ministers. Each minister—with one or two deputies and one appointed secretary—runs several departments, which are divided into divisions and subsections.

A permanent undersecretary is appointed to have administrative control over each ministry. He or she is a career civil servant, responsible for carrying out the policies of the ministry.

Opposite: **The opening of Parliament.**

Below: **The Grand Palace.**

Thai university students demonstrating against a government plan to do business with Japanese corporations.

PROVINCES

The largest and most important ministry is the Ministry of the Interior. It is in charge of the country's public works, rural development, town and country planning, community development, public land, reserved forests, labor affairs, and the police. All local administration comes under this ministry.

Thailand has 73 provinces, each with its own governor who is directly responsible to the Ministry of the Interior. Higher administrative positions at each province are usually filled by officials sent from Bangkok, while those at the lower levels are occupied by locally trained people.

VILLAGES

When King Chulalongkorn improved the provinces' administration, the rural population was organized into *muban*, which means "cluster of houses." (It was easy enough to recognize existing villages as *muban* ["MOO-bahn"] except in the Central Plains, where houses were strung out along canals and divided into "clusters.") Ten to 15 *muban* make up one

tambon ("TAM-bohn").

Each village has an elected headman, who acts as its representative when dealing with the government. For most Thai villages, this has always been the traditional set up. But when hill tribes entered Thailand and were brought under its care, their traditions did not provide for such leaders, so they had to appoint them.

Usually, the tribal headman is selected according to his ability to understand Thai, since his prime duty is to be the middleman between the government and his people. He is usually one of the most industrious and prosperous members of the community and also a person of good moral character who enjoys much respect.

Formerly, all village education came from the local temple compound. Today, the schools are set up outside temples with standardized, secular education. The village schoolteacher has also become an important person. Often, a local person studies at a teacher's training school in a nearby town. The teacher enjoys much honor and his or her opinions on local problems and national affairs are much sought after; it is the teacher who explains the world of politics and related things to the villagers.

The unique courthouse of the city of Chiang Mai. The court system of Chiang Mai is the same as the rest of the country. It is divided into three levels: at the lowest level are the 108 Courts of First Instance or Provincial Courts; the next level is the Uthorn Court or the Court of Appeals; and the highest level is the Dika or Supreme Court. The judgments of the Dika Court are final and only the king has the power to grant appeals after this level.

UPHOLDING THE LAW

Legal cases in Thailand fall under one of the following courts: labor, tax, family, juvenile, military, civil, or criminal. Those unfortunate enough to be arrested are held in the police station, where charges must be filed within three days for minor offenses and within seven for felonies.

The police send the prosecutor a summary of the evidence of the crime, along with their recommendations. The prosecutor then decides the nature of the charge, and if it should be dropped or bail be granted. Bail is set according to the charge and the fines. There is no jury system in Thailand; the judge decides everything. Cases may be appealed based on the verdict or the sentence, although the Court of Appeals may also increase the penalty!

There are no hearings above the Provincial Court, simply a review of the files unless new evidence is produced. There is also a Supreme Court of 52 judges. Three are assigned to each case.

All court activity is slow as hearings take place only once a month. The schedule is especially crowded from November to December. Sentences are usually very heavy. Except for cases of drug and security offenses and slander or insults to the royal family, annual royal pardons reduce the time served.

To become an attorney, a student must pass the bar examination. After three years of practice, the attorney may take another examination to become a judge or prosecutor and then become eligible for promotion to various levels in the national judicial department.

THE ARMY

Potential officers in Thailand's military spend the first two years of service together at a military academy. After this, they can choose their branch of service and attend the appropriate academy for four years.

Since World War II, the military's primary defense activities have focused on breaking up the Communist movement—primarily in the northeast—and fighting a Moslem separatist campaign in the south. In addition, it has had to monitor the border with Myanmar, where a long war between the army and various ethnic groups occasionally spills over onto Thai territory.

But the military's main concern is Thailand's eastern border, where it faces Indochina, a region that has seen decades of unrest, outpourings of thousands of refugees, and other troubles brought by civil war.

The Royal Guards during a colorful ceremony in Bangkok.

Part of the border is patrolled by special local military units. Similar ones operate in the north where, with the Border Patrol Police, they are also involved in the destruction of opium and heroin production and shipment.

The Thai Army has been heavily involved in politics ever since the Revolution of 1932. Most prime ministers since then have been generals and every parliament has included a large faction of retired military officers. But since the demonstrations of May, 1992, the government has taken measures to reduce the army's political influence.

ECONOMY

FOR MANY CENTURIES before King Mongkut opened the country's doors to the West, Thailand's economy was based on agriculture. The people made little use of other resources.

Thailand's economy began to grow after a 1957 government decision to encourage investments. That resulted in a growth of new firms and development in many areas.

The creation in 1959 of a Board of Investment persuaded foreign firms to invest and set up international branches in Thailand.

The United States was the original major investor, but since 1960, Japan has become Thailand's biggest financial and trading partner.

Above: **A jewelry shop in Bangkok's Chinatown. Many of Thailand's hard-working immigrants have succeeded in turning Bangkok into a major center of international business.**

Opposite: **The giant Mab Ta Pud gas plant looks attractive lit up at night.**

Today, traditional Thai products like rice, corn, sugar, cotton, tapioca, tin, rubber, and hardwoods are still the core of Thailand's export business. But today's exports also include canned seafood, frozen shrimp, textiles and clothing, footwear, jewelry, toys, integrated circuits, and electronic component parts.

The country is gradually shifting its emphasis from import to exports, but Thailand's challenge is to keep the economy growing constantly, while protecting a weak agricultural sector, arresting deforestation, and tackling other environmental issues. But it has strong cash reserves, no foreign debt, and a diversified economy. Public confidence is reflected in the Thais increasing amount of cash savings.

Construction workers directing a crane lifting building materials in Bangkok. Many Bangkok residents can still remember that not too long ago many parts of the city were just rice fields. Today, these areas are filled with skyscrapers and apartment and office buildings, a sign of the country's progress.

TOWARD A MODERN ECONOMY

The country's growth has mainly been reflected in the development of its industries and services. In the 1960s, most manufactured goods that filled the shelves of shops in small towns and villages were imported. Today, they are made in Thailand.

The growth in trade has been matched by an improvement in transportation services—new roads and more new buses and trucks. Construction has boomed since the 1960s too, with the rise of new office buildings and housing. Condominiums are popping up everywhere.

At the lower end of the economic scale, there has been the expansion of markets, from the ordinary weekend markets in rural areas to the fancy, multi-level shopping malls in Bangkok, where thousands of stores and vendors ply their goods.

Individual enterprises grow in a country like Thailand. Today, every town has its night market, with countless stalls erected for nighttime shoppers. Including the ever present food stalls, there are over 40,000 of these in Bangkok alone, not to mention 17,000 tailors.

While no part of the country has been untouched by economic development, Bangkok is still the place where fortunes are made. Not merely Thailand's banking capital but also, along with Hong Kong and Singapore, one of the leading financial centers in Southeast Asia, Bangkok is equipped with the latest in communications technology.

OUT ON THE FARMS

Most of Thailand's population are engaged in some form of agricultural work. Rice is the main crop, but its role in the national economy has declined. In 1950, rice accounted for one half of exports; by 1984, it was only 15%.

Currently, the average yields of Thai rice are among the lowest in Asia. Yet its importance goes beyond economics, for not only is it part of nearly every Thai meal; rice is also believed to have a soul of its own, and the various rituals that accompany its cultivation are an integral part of Thai tradition.

A Thai farmer carrying a heavy load of rice stalks on his shoulders. Although Thailand has modern farming equipment, most farmers still perform heavy labor with their own hands.

Agricultural development has not been encouraged in the same way as in the industrial sector, but rivers have been improved and reservoirs built to better serve farming endeavors. In addition, over a thousand "royally-sponsored," small-scale rural projects have been set up to help the agricultural economy.

Development efforts in the farm sector are directed towards increasing grain production. And while farms do not suffer from a labor shortage, poor soil and rainfall patterns block this potential growth area.

The hills and remote jungles are losing trees at a critical rate, mainly to commercial logging. In addition, the hill tribes' practice of slash-and-burn agriculture has further added to deforestation. When an area becomes overpopulated, there are more mouths to feed, more farms are needed, and therefore more trees are cut down. Soil in the hills is difficult to farm, adding to the problem.

The Crocodile Farm is one of Bangkok's favorite tourist attractions. It has more than 30,000 crocodiles, along with tigers, lions, snakes, and elephants.

TOURISM

Besides foreign investment and earnings from exports, Thailand's economy has been boosted by the incredible rise in tourism. Now, five million tourists visit the country yearly, with the figure continuing to rise. Tourism revenue in 1991 totaled 100,004 million baht ($4,000 million), making it more valuable than the exports of textiles, rice, rubber, and tapioca combined.

Besides the services directly connected with tourism, such as hotels, restaurants, and tours, growth in the industry has also restarted the handicraft business. Weavers, embroiderers, carvers, goldsmiths, and other artisans have been turning out everything from traditional craft items to newly-designed souvenirs, utilizing ancient skills that might otherwise have quietly died out.

VANISHING OCCUPATIONS

In the process of changing from a traditional economy to a modern one, many time-honored Thai occupations are being lost. Some are replaced by those with updated techniques, others are abandoned because of a change in available materials or even in consumer demand.

Among those occupations disappearing from the scene are the itinerant dyer, the boat and truck illustrator, the lute player, and the makers of klong jars, monks' wooden begging bowls, theatrical masks and puppets, and granite mortars and pestles.

A herd of elephants crossing a river. The elephant has been an important animal to the Thais for a long time. Many Thais believe it brings them good luck. For example, they believe pregnant women who walk under the belly of an elephant will have easy childbirths.

THE DECLINE OF THE ELEPHANT

Once they were the pride of kings, who rode them in to battle in richly-decorated howdahs (seats on the back of the elephants). White elephants—albino and pinkish—were considered especially grand. King Rama II had one such elephant carry the national flag during ceremonies, and it remained until it was replaced by the present one in 1917.

Back then, elephants had stopped going to war, but were valuable workers in the teak forests, as there is still no way to haul felled logs out of the jungles except by elephant. Elephants pushed the logs together in the rivers to help workers make temporary log rafts to be sent downriver. The logs would take two years to reach Bangkok, but the long period in the water seasoned them into some of the finest hardwoods in the world.

Nowadays the teak business is in decline, partly because of new laws aimed at preserving the forests. Meanwhile, the elephant has been given a more humble role—demonstrating tricks at tourist spots or carrying tourists on short jungle walks in the north.

THAIS

MOST PEOPLE IN THAILAND call themselves Thai, but that is only one of a number of related groups that fall under the generic term Tai (or Dai, as it is spelled in China).

TAIS

Tai origins are hard to pinpoint, as some experts believe they came from northern Sichuan province in China while others claim their first home was southeast China, above Vietnam. About 2,000 years ago, they began calling themselves Tai and migrated south toward Yunnan and Guizhou provinces. What made them move was probably the search for fertile lands or escape from oppressive overlords. But by the seventh or eighth century, some had continued southward into present-day Southeast Asia.

By the 13th century, there were already clear differences among the Tais that were spread over five countries. Today, they are the Black Thais in Vietnam; the Laos, Tai Nueas, and Tai Phuans in Laos; the Tai Lues, Tai Yuans, and Thais in Thailand; the Tai Yais (or Shans) in Myanmar; and the Ahoms in northeastern India. Many other Tai groups continue to reside in southern China, especially in Xishuangbanna, the southernmost district of Yunnan. They all share a common cultural background, and even their textile designs and techniques are similar. While the dialects are not all the same, they do belong to the same language family.

Above: **A troop of Girl Guides line up along a Bangkok sidestreet.**

Opposite: **A Thai woman in her traditional costume.**

A young girl in a boat at the Floating Market. The traditional hat that she wears is uniquely designed to both ward off the sun's heat and allow air to flow better below.

DEMOGRAPHY

Before any of the Tai peoples migrated out of China, Thailand was first settled by Negrito peoples from the south. They pushed up into the heart of present-day Thailand, only to be forced to retreat later by the more powerful Mons and Khmers.

A small number of these early migrants—called the Sakai, Semang, or Ngo—survive in four groups in the southernmost provinces. They are small people who reside in the jungles, using blowpipes for hunting. Eleven other groups live in Malaysia.

Meanwhile, the Mons are hardly a separate people any longer in Thailand, after being conquered by the Khmers, Thais, and Burmese, although they still have a strong community in Myanmar. The racial purity of Thailand's people has been mixed by war and long periods of living together. During the Ayutthaya period, the victors of major wars between Siam, Burma, Chiang Mai, Luang Prabang, or Kampuchea took hundreds of thousands of prisoners back to their countries. This helps account for the great racial diversity among the Thais.

With the end of the Burmese wars, Thailand became the destination of new peoples on the move—the hill tribes of neighboring countries. First it was the Karens from the west. Then, from the beginning of the 20th century, tribes from Laos, Myanmar, Yunnan, and Guizhou started arriving. Most of them have settled in the north, where the hills and forests resemble the lands they left behind.

SINO-THAIS AND THAI MOSLEMS

The Chinese make up the largest minority group in Thailand—just over 10% of the population. Coming from southern China, the migration was at its greatest from 1860 to 1940. Of all the Chinese in Southeast Asia, those in Thailand have been absorbed the most into local society.

When the Chinese came to work or set up businesses, they had to learn Thai rather than colonial tongues, and they became Buddhists while not abandoning their ancestral worship and customs. Today's Chinese-Thais or Sino-Thais observe Buddhist rites and respect the importance of kin groups, but speak Thai and follow most Thai customs. After World War II, laws that discriminated against Sino-Thais were repealed, which prompted them to keep their money in Thailand rather than send it back to China.

Thai Moslems, whether the half-million ethnic Thais or the 1.5 million Malays in the south, have been less-assimilated. Most are Sunni Moslems living in fishing communities, which keeps them out of mainstream Thai society. Their children usually attend Islamic schools, for conservative parents object to the dress code and customs of the other schools. In general, they feel uncomfortable under a non-Moslem government, yet have shown little support for separatist movements.

One interesting tribe living in Nan Province, where Thailand shares borders with Laos and Myanmar, is the Phi Tong Luang or "spirits of the yellow leaves." They are a very small nomadic tribe. Their title derives from their habit of moving whenever the leaves with which they make their huts turn yellow.

A Bangkok family in a bus after it was caught in a sudden rainstorm. Bangkok regularly gets flooded during the annual monsoon; just a half-hour of rain can change the roads into small rivers. But even the Thais are not always this cheerful when heavy rain hits. One of the worst rainfalls occurred in 1983, when floods damaged Bangkok so much that the bill to rebuild the city was over 6.5 billion baht ($260 million)!

PEOPLE OF THE ISAN

People of the northeast—the Isan—call themselves Laos and speak a dialect closer to that of their relatives in Laos than that of the Thais. At the end of the 19th century, this region split into dozens of small states run by lords who paid tribute to the king of Siam. The northeast has suffered from a sense of distance, both physical and political, from Bangkok and its strange weather patterns. These factors have blocked the northeast's development.

Most Laos are farmers—often tenant farmers—and followers of old customs. Many migrate to Bangkok and other towns during the dry season and work in services and small factories.

Besides the Laos, there are also about 700,000 ethnic Khmers and 250,000 Kuis, a related group, in the Isan. Most live near the Kampuchean border.

TRADITIONAL COSTUMES

Traditional Thai clothing was not tailored to fit a person exactly. Instead, it was made of narrow strips of woven silk or cotton that were joined, folded, or tucked to serve as various garments.

For women, the basic costume was a *pha sin* ("Pah Sin"), which was two or three strips of cloth sewn into a tube that is worn around the waist and tucked in at the navel. Another narrow strip was wrapped around the chest, although while working, they left their breasts bare. Men wore a strip that was tied between their legs and around the waist. Both men and women carried their belongings in cloth shoulder bags.

Pha sin can be plain, but were usually striped in patterns that identified with a location or ethnic group. Often, the lower cloths were specially embroidered.

Nineteenth century Thai monarchs encouraged changes in the Thai dress, preferring a more Western look. Men started wearing shirts, and for both sexes, tailored clothes became fashionable.

After World War II, the government promoted a complete changeover to Western clothing. Now the *pha sin* is regarded as the dress of the poor or the stubbornly traditional. It is seen mainly in villages or at festival parades.

A young Thai Lue couple posing in their ethnic tribal costumes.

HILL TRIBES

Hill tribes in the north make their villages out of jungle materials and practice the most ancient method of agriculture—the slash-and-burn method.

Every winter, farmers clear a patch of forest, then burn the felled trees and shrubs. The ashes fertilize the otherwise poor soil enough to grow rice and other crops for one or two years. They then abandon that field and start all over again on a new one. They return to the original patch after several years, leaving it for the annual monsoons to feed the returning vegetation.

A Meo family during their evening meal. Sitting around at tribal get-togethers and meals is done on the floor. The meal is always rice (once in a while it is noodles). But around the rice bowl are dishes of vegetables that the mother has spent the whole morning peeling, pounding, scraping, or chopping.

Hill tribes left their original homelands because of wars and rebellions. In Myanmar and Laos, they found they did not have the space to grow rice successfully. So they turned to growing opium, which can be grown on the same field for 10 years, as a cash crop to barter for their rice. This became a huge Thai problem when tribes, fleeing new wars and ethnic unrest in Myanmar and Laos, began moving into secluded Thai forests and, in some cases, continuing the opium business.

The Thai government began taking action against this in 1976, and today most opium farmers have been persuaded to raise other crops instead. Still, increasing immigration across the borders has put a strain on the area. This has prompted the government to begin reforestation projects, introduce stricter border controls, and even throw out or relocate whole groups of people.

A young Akha girl embroidering. In their free time most Akha women embroider their black shirts and hats with bright cloth beads and silver ornaments. Considered the most backward of all the hill tribes, Akha women, however, were more advanced than anyone else in one area of fashion: they were wearing miniskirts long before it became popular in the West!

Thai teenagers gathering to have fun during the Songkran waterthrowing festival.

INDIVIDUAL TRIBES

The **Karens** number 265,000 and make up half the hill tribes. They usually live on hills with elavations of 1,650 feet, but also have farms in the plains. Karens are spread out along Thailand's western border.

The **Meos** or **Hmongs** total 80,000. One of the largest southern Chinese ethnic groups, they entered Thailand via Laos and have spread to 13 provinces. Their women wear skirts of *batik* cloth, and both sexes favor brightly-embroidered costumes. Meo customs reflect their Chinese origins.

There are 35,000 **Yaos** or **Miens**. Also from southeastern China, the Yaos are the most Chinese of all the originally Chinese tribes in Thailand. They even use Chinese characters for their songs and stories. The women wear fully-embroidered pants and black turbans.

The **Lahus** or **Musurs** number 60,000. Originating from Yunnan, they are divided into six groups and wear different costumes. Many are converting to Christianity, although most still worship a variety of gods.

There are 33,000 **Akhas**. Originally from Yunnan, via Myanmar, they live on ridges of about 3,000 to 5,000 foot elevation. Their villages are distinguished by a pair of gates and a large swing, and their women wear distinctive heavy, silver-laden headdresses and beautiful jackets.

The **Lisus** total 25,000. Also from Yunnan, they reside on hillsides 3,000 feet high. Their culture displays some Chinese influence. They are a very competitive people. Lisu women wear bright tunics with striped shoulders.

Various other smaller groups of hill tribes include the Mon-Khmer people like the **Lawas** and, in the province of Nan, the **Htins** and **Khamus**. A few dozen forest-dwelling **Mlabris**—the most primitive of all the tribes— round off the population.

THE REFUGEES

Thailand has been more than a nervous witness to the wars in the neighboring region of Indochina. From 1975 to 1980, war, famine, and political terror prompted over a million people to flee Laos, Kampuchea, and Vietnam into refugee camps along the Thai border, hoping to resettle there or in Western countries. The United Nations has set up two agencies to help Thailand maintain the camps. But some 250,000 Thais who used to live along the border were themselves displaced by the refugees. There followed battles between Khmer liberation fighters (like the one pictured right) and the Kampuchean army. Stray artillery shells in such fights often cause much damage to homes and heavy loss of life. With the winding down of Kampuchea's civil war, Khmer refugees have gone home. But a new outbreak of violence could send them fleeing once again.

LIFESTYLE

DESPITE THE PRESENCE of cosmopolitan cultures in Thailand's cities and in parts of the countryside, social and even professional life is still characterized by observing a set of values and by behavior rooted in Thai tradition. Still, modernization brings rapid changes into Thai society; new social classes rise and old ones decline.

But the principles of behavior remain the same. Thais believe in a "Thai Way" of doing things; this ensures that, come what may, the harmony that is necessary for a good life will be maintained. To understand this, let us start with a few basic points.

Jai yen ("jai-YEN") means "cool heart," and this is the key quality demanded in all social gatherings. It means the ability to accept most things with grace and calm. Its opposite, always considered a social wrong, is any showing of *jai rohn* ("jai-ROHN"), a "hot heart." Anger, impatience, and visible displeasure are examples.

Krengjai ("KREN-jai") is translated as "consideration," but it specifically means a demonstration of consideration for the feelings of others, particularly one's superiors. As such, *krengjai* contains the notions of humility, politeness, respect, and obedience. This ideal principle is stressed throughout every Thai's up-bringing, and is important in all Thai social behavior.

Opposite: **One of Bang-kok's many multi-leveled shopping centers. Shopping is a pleasure in Thailand, not just because of the wide variety of things but also for the low prices. Besides the fine Thai silk, shoppers buy lots of jewelry, handicrafts, antiques, bronzeware, and children's dolls.**

Below: **An unusual sight for foreigners, but to the average Thai an elephant on the street is common. Despite this, transportation by the gentle giants is slowly declining.**

Practical

Casual

Carefree

Shy

Ways to wear a *pakama* (headpiece)

THAI SOCIETY

Today's Thailand is both modern and traditional. In the present world, institutions and laws ensure that advancing in society is possible for anyone with ambition and talents. But Thai culture has old and deep roots, and traditional Thai society is established in customs and attitudes that are centuries old.

Thais believe they are born into a place in society that is determined by the *karma* ("KAHR-mah")—the effects of thought and deed—of their past lives. However, for their acts of *tham boon* ("tahm BOON")—making merit—they can advance their social position.

Despite this, there will always be people they deal with who are of higher or lower status. And this must be acknowledged by proper speech and the relevant gestures and actions appropriate to the given social situation. Thus, for most Thais, there are always superiors to respect, meaning people who are given special treatment because of their higher status.

THAI WAY

Restraint and courtesy are the focal points of Thai social relations. The language of both speech and gesture features these qualities. Even in greeting one another, Thais indicate status, for the type of greeting used depends on the rank of the person addressed.

Gestures used by those of lower ranks automatically recognize the status of the higher ranks. The most complex gestures are reserved for the royal family or Buddhist monks.

Those automatically given respect—that is, those who are recognized as of higher social rank—include patrons, employers, teachers, parents, grandparents and, in general, anyone older. The superior returns a simpler greeting that acknowledges the respect given. The conversation, if there is one, proceeds according to the principles of *krengjai* and *jai yen*.

The Thai Way discourages individuals from being blunt or outspoken. Thais view these as socially bad traits, a threat to harmony. The Thai use of pronouns reflects this. The Thai language book used at Bangkok's American University Alumni lists 11 different words for "you." But in ordinary conversation, Thais usually avoid "you" and use the addressee's name instead. Nor do they use the word "I," unless absolutely necessary.

We must remember that the extraordinary attention given to keeping the social harmony came from a village-based culture. The economy of a village often required all villagers to cooperate and help in such matters as rice planting and harvesting, flood control and relief, and other projects. Individual concerns were always second to the interests of the community. Harmony governed life.

Religious beliefs also support this. *Jai rohn* actions are considered by most Thais to be a challenge to household spirits, who would then punish the guilty party for the disturbance.

The Thai Way also provides guidelines for handling conflicts and criticism. Both *jai yen* and *krengjai* come into play here. A Thai will never criticize a superior directly; not just because of the loss of face, but because it would challenge the superior's right to be obeyed. Criticism, and therefore changes, must be done behind the scenes.

The young lady is demonstrating the proper way to serve something to someone who is older, while the young man keeps his head bowed when passing someone his senior. Thai people show much respect for the older generation in everything they do.

The "wai" ("wai") is the Thai greeting sign that most foreigners recognize. It is made by raising both hands, palms joined, to lightly touch the body between the chest and forehead, something like the praying action. The higher the hands are raised, the greater the respect is given; and the junior person always gives the "wai" before the senior (for an older person to "wai" the younger first is considered bad luck). In general, the "wai" may be done standing, sitting, walking, or even on the sickbed.

THE SMILE

The Thai codes of behavior, based on restraint and courtesy, discourage a hearty belly laugh, but Thais do smile a lot. Amusement and expressing thanks are two obvious reasons to smile.

Thais also tend to smile in order to side-step difficult questions, to excuse any lack of courtesy, and to cover their embarrassment. They do not smile to appreciate ironies, though, and have virtually no sense of black humor. But the readiness with which Thais smiles is one of the more charming aspects of the Thai Way.

FAMILY

In Thai society, the immediate family is much more important than the extended family. And the mother's side of the family rates higher than the father's, especially in the north and northeast. Thais do not form kinship groups as found in Chinese and Indian societies, and extended family ties are not as important.

But within the immediate family, Thais are very close to one another. Relationships are based on the younger generation honoring and obeying the older generation, and appearing humble before them. Younger siblings obey older brothers and sisters, while the older ones assume responsibility for the behavior of the younger ones.

Thai women play vital roles within the family and in the community, for they nurture their own children and provide food for the community's monks when the monks' make their morning rounds.

Most Thai men, unfortunately, do not recognize women as their social equals, an attitude that has permitted the tolerance of prostitution and the *mia noi* ("mee-a NOI")—the "minor wife" or concubine.

A hill tribe mother and her two children. The family is the cornerstone of Thai society. There is a real feeling of togetherness among family members. If any member of the family is in some sort of trouble, the rest of the family gives up everything to help; if one is ill, someone in the family will always be there to help look after him or her. This love and respect is called *oonjai,* or "heartwarming." It is usually a sense of security that one has. Thai mothers like the one pictured here will never have to worry about their old age; they know that their children will always be there to take care of them, to love and support them.

Thais give their newborn babies cloths with the drawings of a giant to protect them from evil spirits. This giant, Taowetsuwan, is a famous personality in Thai myths. Legend says that Taowetsuwan was offering food to monks one day and spilled some hot liquid onto a monk's foot. As the monk yelped in pain, Taowetsuwan just stood there laughing. For this, he was sent to the world of the giants. Even though he became king, he suffered much because his feet constantly felt as if hot liquid was being poured onto them.

BIRTHS

For educated Thais, there are scores of magazines and books to consult for the latest medical information. But in the rural areas, many folks still believe it is the spirits (*phi*—"pee") who make the child. They believe that within three days of the birth, the *phi* will come to view the baby, and if they like it, they will take it away.

People will try to please these spirits with tiny food offerings on a platter made from banana leaves or the sheaths of a plantain stem, hoping that this will make them leave the baby alone.

Meanwhile, no one should compliment the mother on the baby's fine appearance, or else the spirits will overhear and become more determined to snatch the child. If all the appropriate steps are followed and all goes well, then, on the fourth day, the child belongs to its parents.

But for the first month a child is not considered a family member, a custom perhaps dating back to earlier times when infants frequently died before a month had passed. After the first month, in a special rite, the child becomes the happy family's son or daughter.

Thais pamper their children when they are young, indulging them and satisfying their every whim. Pampering is so widespread that social critics have charged that although the practice produces well-behaved and contented children, it retards their ability to make decisions on their own and to think critically.

GROWING UP

Most children start elementary school at the age of six or seven. The indulging stage is now over and they are expected to become more self-sufficient and to take on small responsibilities. Still, a bit of pampering continues, and it is common to see adults giving up their seats to schoolchildren on the bus.

Traditionally, boys retain a knot of hair on top of their heads while they are growing; there is an old belief that it wards off illness. At the age of 11 or 13 (never an even number), they undergo complete haircuts in a public ceremony staged in January.

In the first three years of elementary school, children are taught basic Thai language skills, are introduced to math and science, and learn music and drawing. They learn a lot of songs at this age as well. In their fourth year, they will begin learning Thai history; the following year will see them studying world history, geography, religion, and literature.

Six years of elementary school is required for all Thai children. Consequently, Thailand has one of the most literate populations in the world. Six years of high school are possible next, but this is neither compulsory nor free, so it is mainly urban dwelling children who go to high school, and even fewer who go on to universities.

Technical and vocational schools are alternatives to attending ordinary high schools. For those who do go beyond elementary schools, military training begins in the ninth grade. Drills dominate the first two years, after which boys are taught the use of firearms.

A Thai English teacher and her class. Besides the temple, the public school is the most important building in the Thai village. It is the symbol of progress and provides the children with a sense of purpose.

This happy couple being married kneels inside a semicircle, each wearing a crown of looped white yarn called a *mongkol*. The two *mongkols* are joined by a string to symbolize the uniting of the man and woman as husband and wife.

MARRIAGE

Young Thai men and women, except royalty and conservative Moslems, choose partners for themselves. Although they would prefer their parents' approval, they may proceed without it. There are many opportunities for young men to meet the opposite sex, for young women are allowed to grow up and socialise in mixed company.

Traditional Thai attitudes to marriage are changing, as most people get married nowadays at a much later age than their parents and grandparents, except in the more remote rural areas. Many young women are postponing marriage in favor of a career. It is no longer unusual to meet bright and beautiful women who are over 30 years old and unmarried.

Traditional Thai marriages are usually performed by as many as nine

Buddhist monks. The ceremony begins in the morning with the happy couple wearing headdresses joined by a white thread. Monks place a white cord, called a *sai sin*, around the area that the couple are standing on, marking it off as a sacred zone. A half-hour of chanting and blessing follows, and the senior monk sprinkles holy water over the couple, using a sprig of Chinese gooseberry.

In the evening, purified water is poured over the joined hands of the bride and groom. After a rousing wedding party, the next event is a trip to the bride's house. In former times, the groom was required to build a house for himself and his bride in his father-in-law's compound. Nowadays, he merely presents gifts to the bride's family. Generally, the party has to pass through "toll gates" erected by the children at the bride's house, who ask for money.

Among the hill tribes and upcountry villages, marriages are often more elaborate. Here, they may not marry within the same clan. Among Akhas, there must be seven generations without a common ancestor. Among Meos, couples must be roughly the same age, or at least not so much as a generation apart.

Tribal marriage negotiations revolve around such things as a proper "bride price" (among Yaos), terms of gifts and services (among Lisus), or how long the groom will live with the bride's family (a Karen custom). The actual ceremony finds the couple dressed in grand costumes and the bride playing the role of a shy maiden.

Among most tribes, the costume of an unmarried woman differs from a married one, so it is easy to know whom to court. Funerals and weddings, which usually draw a crowd, are ideal opportunities. Most rural and tribal folk get married sometime between New Year's Day and the planting of the annual rice crop in late spring or early summer.

Most Thai marriages take place in even-numbered lunar months. This is because weddings involve two people, so the wedding months should be multiples of two. The best lunar months are the second, fourth, sixth or eighth. However, the 10th or the 12th month are not chosen, while the ninth month is, simply because the number nine is associated with progress and wealth in Thailand.

Motorcycles are very popular among younger Thai men.

CAREER

For young Thais with ambition, 12 years of school is not enough and they will try to gain admission into one of the 16 state and 27 private colleges and universities.

The oldest and most famous of these are the Chulalongkorn and Thammasat Universities, both in Bangkok. The latter was founded in 1934 after the revolution. Entrance to both of these is very difficult, whereas admission to some of the other universities is less competitive, and class attendance there is voluntary.

The government recruits its officers from among the graduates of Chulalongkorn or Thammasat, as do top corporations, usually after the student has gone abroad to acquire a master's degree.

However, Thai society is very biased about who will be chosen. The civil service wants graduates from "a socially acceptable family," while newspaper advertisements for managerial candidates state that applicants must have "good social connections."

Besides government service and business, other professions rated highly by Thai society include bankers and stock brokers, engineers and technical specialists, doctors, judges, monks, hotel managers, pilots, and—especially among rural folk—military or police officers.

FREE TIME

Being a friendly people, Thais do not like to spend their free time alone, and often cannot understand how others could. School teaches them to enjoy the company of others and often holidays are spent in group outings, such as trips to natural or historical sites.

As they get older, this continues. Thais like to eat out. Not that they dislike cooking but because they enjoy the social scene. Office workers and student groups often organize picnics or weekend seaside trips, and the zest for joining the crowd peaks at weddings, funerals, and other ceremonies.

Urban folk have all the usual distractions available in the cities—television, movie theaters, bars, discos, night clubs, concerts, shopping malls, night markets, and so forth. Those in the countryside do not have such options, although cinemas and video recorders seemed to have spread everywhere. There are also 269 radio stations throughout the country, with some broadcasting in dialects or tribal languages.

In remote areas like hill villages, the main fun activity is visiting friends and relatives. Unique to the Akhas is a designated place where young singles meet, sing, dance, and amuse themselves.

Whenever Thais have nothing to do, they love to "pai tio," or hang around some place with no particular aim except to enjoy the fresh air or watch people. Whenever you see Thais walking slowly and looking around, chances are they are going "pai tio." Thais love to watch people, and to see people, you have to "pai tio." The best places to "pai tio" are marketplaces, religious festivals, and theaters.

Some Thais cremate their dead in beautifully-designed structures.

DEATHS

When Thais are ill, they can choose from among several types of remedies. Aside from the variety of drugs and treatments available in the markets, they may try either Thai or Chinese traditional herbal medicine. The former is mild and slow-acting, the latter sharp but quite effective.

Death can't always be avoided, of course, but Thai Buddhists believe in an afterlife and reincarnation. When a person dies at home, the corpse is kept three to seven days before it is removed. If death occurs elsewhere, the remains are taken directly to a temple to be cremated within a week.

Funerals are occasions that Buddhists believe can be used to improve the existence in this life and the next. Consequently, they are usually as lavish as the wealth of a family will permit, involving many gifts, feasting, and a film or theater presentation.

When the day is selected (never a Friday), the family of the deceased bathes, perfumes, dresses, and lays the corpse out on a mat. They place a one-baht coin in the mouth, fold the hands into a *wai*, tie them with white thread, and insert into the palms a banknote, two flowers, and two candles. Then they tie the ankles, seal the mouth and eyes with wax, and put the body into a coffin with the head facing west, the direction the dead should face according to tradition.

Next to the head of the coffin, the family lights a lamp, while beside it they place a sleeping mat, blanket, plates, food, clothing, and a knife for use in the afterlife. Guests donate banknotes, which are fixed onto bamboo sticks and planted like flags in the side of the coffin. Monks chant for three days beside the corpse, taking meals in the home of the deceased. At the end of the session, the coffin is carried feet first out of the house. The ladder to the house is reversed and the water jar is turned upside down, actions designed to discourage the soul from trying to re-enter the home.

On the way to the cremation site, mourners scatter grains of rice to soothe the deceased's spirit. Memorial services are held after three months and again at the one-year anniversary of the death.

Most ethnic minorities, such as the Moslems and nearly all hill tribal groups, bury their dead instead of cremating them.

Funerals in the villages can be quite grand events, with the whole village turning up and participating. Some tribes have special, highly-decorated costumes that are worn only during funerals. Buffaloes or cattle are slaughtered and the meat divided among either the clan of the deceased or the entire village.

The dead person's family is dressed in light-colored clothing and sackcloth at a traditional Chinese funeral.

Ban Bang Lee, a town near Nakhon Pathom, looks like any other town in Thailand. But as you enter it, the road dips sharply down. The whole town actually lies in a crater-like hollow. Every building has at least two floors, but—unlike the usually airy and openly constructed style of most Thai houses—the first floor is completely closed off. Why? Because during the rainy season the lower part of the town is completely waterlogged. The roads suddenly disappear into a lake. The people substitute their cars for boats and carry on with their lives as if nothing had happened.

THAI HOUSES

The traditional Thai house is made of strong hardwoods and stands on poles, with the living quarters raised above the ground. Since half the year is wet and damp, this is an altogether healthy living arrangement. The space beneath the living quarters is left open, and in dry weather it serves as a work place, especially for weaving.

The upper floor of the rectangular building consists of an L-shaped terrace, a sheltered verandah, and the main house, which is generally divided into a receiving-dining room and the sleeping quarters.

Shoes are removed and left at the stairs on the ground floor, where there may also be a water jar and dipper for a person to clean up before entering. The upper floor is often swept and washed down, for Thais in general are extremely clean; they take daily baths and are constantly cleaning their homes.

The house itself sits in a compound along with smaller buildings. All are usually surrounded by a wall. The area that houses the grain and rice-pounding shed is separate from the house, while the kitchen and water-storage room are attached to the main building. Thais in the Central Plains draw their water from rivers and *klong*, while those in the north and northeast rely on artesian wells.

One more building completes the Thai house—the spirit house. This resembles a miniature temple mounted on a stand. Small offerings are regularly left around the spirit house for the protecting spirit of the compound. They usually include flowers, food, and incense. This is a custom that illustrates Thailand's pre-Buddhist roots.

In the countryside, a farmer's hut is usually made of palm thatch, sticks, and straws tightly stacked around a tall stout pole that is sunk deep into the ground. It is every bit as steady as a regular Thai house!

The average Thai home is a mixture of simple designs and elegant architecture. The first thing you will notice is how clean, neat, and cozy it is. The finer houses are made of carved and polished teakwood, with tiled roofs. Local astrologers will determine the best time for groung breaking, erecting the walls and roof, and positioning each step that leads up to the house. Then the owners will call in the local monks to give whatever blessings that are necessary to make sure the house has an auspicious beginning. Sometimes owners will wait for weeks before putting up the walls, windows, or doors. That is, until the astrologers or monks tell them it is time. Then large numbers of friends and relatives will gather to help do the job in real Thai style, complete with a celebration and feast at the end of the day.

RELIGION

THE MAJORITY OF THAIS ARE BUDDHISTS. Buddhism, with the state and the monarchy, is one of the three official "pillars" of the nation. The king is considered the protector of all religions, so there is religious freedom dating back to the early 17th century, when Ayutthaya kings permitted Christians to build churches.

Buddhism only became the state religion during the kingdom of Sukhothai. At that time, Thai settlers already had the sophisticated religion of the Mons and Khmers. Through them, the Thais adopted the Hindu view of kingship, the caste system of the Brahmins, and the worship of Erawan, the elephant god. Hindu influence can also be seen in classic literature, such as the story of Rama and Sita in the *Ramakien,* the Thai version of the *Ramayana.*

Thais, before such cultural contact, practiced animism or the worship of natural objects. To them, the world was filled with invisible *phi* that must be pleased lest they upset life's harmony. In many parts of the country, dealing with the *phi* requires more attention than carrying out Buddhist rites.

Relations with the *phi* dominated tribal religion as well. These tribes also practiced Chinese ancestor worship, performing acts of merit at temples to ask for help in fighting the evil *phi,* whom they blame for all of their agricultural problems.

Opposite and below: **Buddhist monks play an important part in the history of Thailand and the lives of many of its people.**

The fat Chinese god of wealth is a very popular figure in Thailand. Here, worshipers toss coins to its large navel; many Thai Chinese believe that this will bring them good luck and fortune.

PRE-BUDDHISM

Another ancient Thai religious personality is the *khwan* ("kwahn"), a vital spirit that sometimes possesses lifeless things.

Thais believe there are 32 such *khwan* in the human body, and the most important one is in the head. This *khwan* is said to be very sensitive to bad behavior, and the slightest insult will make it leave. It can only be called back with a special ritual. (This accounts for Thai sensitivity about being touched or hit on the head.) All such beliefs were absorbed into the newly-adopted state religion of Buddhism. The Thai form of Buddhism, called Theravada, originated from Sinhalese monks in Thailand, Myanmar, Laos, and Kampuchea. It is specifically characterized by a large body of monks—called the Sangha—staying in temple compounds, from which all Thai art, crafts, and learning originated. The Sangha is supported by donations from Buddhists who believe such acts will decrease their suffering in this life or the next.

Between the 13th and 15th century, the Sangha became the central religious institution in Thai society. By the time of King Mongkut, many non-Buddhist practices had crept in. Under King Chulalongkorn, a standard system of education for monks was created and, in 1902, the Sangha was united under one leadership.

BUDDHIST PRACTICES

Buddhists believe that suffering exists because of desire and attachment, and to eliminate this, they go through the Eightfold Path. The strictest followers of this are the monks.

Most monks in a monastery are novices, but some have chosen to make a career of it. They can assure themselves of social advancement if they get through the higher religious schools. For a rural youth from an average background, the monastery is a way to a better life, and if he is not committed to his religious position, he can leave the monkhood at any time.

Monks follow a tough code of regulations. They depend totally on the community for support, making the rounds with their bowls early each morning, begging for food. They chant mornings and evenings, attend readings and other rites, study the ancient texts, and retire and wake up early to start the day again.

Monks are involved in all aspects of Thai life, and even bless buildings under construction. But it is not necessary to employ a monk for other acts of devotion.

Young Buddhist monks doing homework on the monastery floor.

Thais make trips to the temple whenever they feel the urge or the necessity. Their offerings are usually jasmine flowers and incense sticks. Sometimes they dab some gold leaf onto statues of the Buddha.

Nearby, captured fish or birds are sold. Buddhists buy them to release as acts of merit. Occasionally, a Buddhist may hire a troupe of temple dancers, either to ask for a favor or to give thanks to a god.

In Thailand, animism (the worship of spirits within objects) and Buddhism are combined in many ways. For instance, children from Buddhist families often wear charms on their arms or legs to ward off evil spirits. Thai Buddhists do not seem to care whether the charm is a Buddhist amulet or one prepared by the village witch doctor. Thai Buddhists take no chances; they may consider them- selves Buddhists, but they do not want to "offend the spirits."

SUMMER AT THE *WAT*

Some years before the fall of Sukhothai, one of the monarchs, King Lithai, temporarily left his throne in order to spend some time as a monk. He thereby started a custom that has been followed by Thai men ever since. Every male is expected to spend a few months in a monastery, or *wat*, and the most popular time for this is during the last three months of the rainy season—the Buddhist Lent.

Thais believe there are several benefits to this. If a boy becomes a novice monk, his mother will not enter Hell; if he becomes a full monk, his father will also not enter Hell. Government servants who elect to spend a summer in a *wat* receive full pay during their stay. But the real benefit supposedly lies in the study of Buddhist teachings. A stint in a monastery is expected to remind the monks of the laws of Buddhism.

OTHER RELIGIONS

While most Chinese are Theraveda Buddhists, they also practice ancestor worship and pray to favorite gods from the Taoist and Mahayana Buddhist traditions. Chinese temples display ancestral tablets on decorated altars. Often, these shrines are dedicated to specific legendary Chinese heroes or heroines.

THE GENEROUS PRINCE

Of all the stories in Thai religious literature, the most popular one is that of Prince Vessandorn, an incarnation of the Buddha.

In the story, Vessandorn gives away the country's prized white elephant to foreigners to relieve their land of drought. But because of this, his own people demand his exile. So he departs, giving away his possessions—even his children—as he goes. The god Indra at one point tricks Vessandorn into giving his wife to him, but later he returns her to the prince. After some complications, Vessandorn is recalled by his father and reunited with his children.

The tale portrays Vessandorn as a role model for important relationships, generosity, and religious merit. It is recited every year at the *wat* on full moon nights at the end of the Buddhist Lent.

Chinese festivals are usually more confusing than those of the Thais. In the south, Chinese events can become occasions for strange acts of self-mutilation and walking on hot coals.

Thailand's Moslems live in the southern provinces. Pattani alone has 515 mosques. Conservative Moslems object to the dress codes of most schools and send their children to religious or vocational Islamic schools. Moslem children who attend Thai schools and follow the prescribed dress code, also attend weekly Islamic religious instruction.

Hill tribes usually practice their own religions, which are closely tied in with their agricultural life. Like the Chinese, they honor their ancestors. The Meos and Yaos follow several other Chinese or Daoist customs.

Efforts to convert these tribes to Buddhism have met with no success. However, Christianity has influenced up to a third of most tribal groups, partly because many of them were already Christians before they came from Myanmar, and partly because of the work of Thai Christians and foreign missionaries. The small but rapidly growing Christian community resides mainly in the north.

Christianity has played a minor but important role in Thailand. Christian missionaries helped educate King Mongkut, who opened the country to the West. They also started the first printing press and newspapers, and introduced modern medical practices and schools.

Telling fortunes by reading the "signs" or lines on the palm is big business in Thailand. According to Thai fortune tellers, there are three major "lines" that all people have, called the "president lines," which consist of the heart line, the head line, and the life line. A long life line means long life; heart lines that are not continuous mean there will be trouble for the heart; and a long head line means intelligence.

FORTUNE TELLING

Like most countries, Thailand has its share of fortune tellers. The most popular ones use a deck of 32 cards. He or she assigns one to the client, then lays the rest of the cards around it and interprets the arrangement.

Palmistry is also common. If a palmist has the client's astrological birth information (especially the time), he or she claims to be able to predict the future by reading the lines on the palms. Sometimes they even take a palmprint to better check all the tiny branch lines.

Experts say there are major lines that represent the head, heart, life, fate, success, and so forth, and that the patterns can reveal both the present and the future.

THAI ASTROLOGY

In Old Siam, it was the astrologer's duty to fix the time for a military battle or attack to begin. Thai armies changed the color of their battle outfits depending on which color was favorable for that day.

Astrology is still taken seriously for ceremonies in Thailand. Events from state rituals to the laying of foundation stones must always begin at a precise time. That is also a task for astrologers to determine. They read horoscopes to determine the suitability of prospective marriage partners, or even to advise for or against business investments.

MIND AND BODY THERAPY

Life within the walls of temples is more active than one would think. Some time is given to meditation, but this is usually practiced by forest monks who stay far away from the outside world. Unlike India with its yoga, or Japan with its Zen, Thailand does not have any traditional meditation exercises.

It does, however, have a practice (derived from a variety of Eastern traditions) thought to have been introduced in the second or third century B.C., involving invisible energy lines running throughout the body. Students of Thai massage, usually taught at the temples (particularly at Wat Po in Bangkok), are instructed on how to apply pressure at several points of the body in order to distribute the patient's "energy flow" more evenly. This is said to relieve stress.

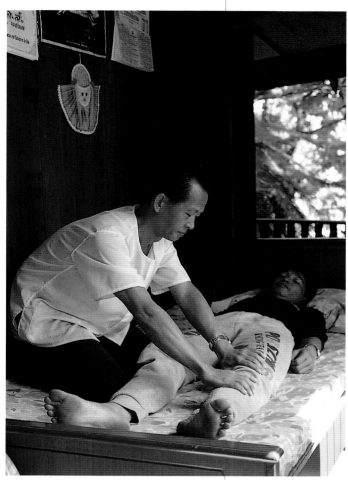

Massage is a traditional therapy in Thailand.

Two young women presenting an offering of flowers before the statue of a Thai saint in Chiang Mai.

AMULETS

In prehistoric times, people's creative response to evil spirits was to invent magical devices to defend themselves. Additionally, they considered certain rare trees, plants, or animals beneficial because they believed friendly spirits resided in them. They believed that parts of these objects could represent spirits, and when worn or mounted in one's house, they protected the owner from unseen evils. In Thailand, despite seven centuries of Buddhism, such practices continue.

Almost every Thai male—and many women—wears or carries some sort of amulet. Some wear as many as 10 at a time to protect themselves from every imaginable harm, from accidents to gunfire to snakebites.

Makers of amulets have adopted symbols of other religions. It is quite common to find people wearing amulets of figures like the Buddha and other religious images, on votive tablets, pendants or famous monks, yantra cloths, and mantras written in Khmer letters stuffed into tiny cylinders to be worn around the neck. Other amulets include stones and seeds, tiger teeth, and boar tusks.

Many such charms may be purchased from stands set up either near popular temples or on busy market streets. Some, like special mantras, must be obtained from "spirit doctors" or "trance mediums" who can recommend the type of talisman required. There are even regular publications of stories about amulets, and articles with expert advice on how to tell a real amulet from a false one. There are also stories of wearers who have survived horrible experiences because of their charms.

The most permanent sort of amulet is the mantra tattooed onto the body—usually on the chest or arms—and always done in Khmer lettering. Rituals accompany the work, intended either to promote healing or to prevent harm from spirits. This sort of tattooing is popular in the north and northeast, among both Thais and other tribal groups.

A different kind of body decoration existed in the past among northern men. They underwent an operation for several days that left them completely tattooed from the waist to the kneecaps. It was considered a test of their manly abilities to withstand the pain. This custom was adopted from their ethnic cousins, the Shans.

In 1770, the Burmese king who controlled that region ordered all males to be tattooed. The order never reached most of the country and so neither did the custom. The temple murals of the north show many tattooed males wearing loin cloths. This was to show off the bold, dark-blue patterns on their thighs to admiring ladies.

The fierce *yak*, found in many temples, is said to scare away evil spirits.

LANGUAGE

THE NATIONAL LANGUAGE OF THAILAND, taught in all schools, is the Central Plains dialect of Thai, also known as Siamese Thai, or even Bangkok Thai to upcountry folks. Although nearly everyone in the country has at least some knowledge of this dialect, many Thais—even ethnic Thais—speak different dialects.

Altogether, standard Thai and Thai dialects are the mother tongues of about 84% of the population. Chinese (that is, the Teochew dialect), is the language of about 10%.

Mon-Khmer speakers make up 3%, the greatest portion being Kampuchean, followed by Kui, Mon, Lawa, Htin, and Khamu. Malays in the south speak the Yawi dialect of the Malay language and account for about another 3%.

Above: **A couple talking. It is rude in Thailand to show the soles of your feet to anybody. As a result, women sit with their feet behind them and men with their legs crossed.**

Opposite: **The stone monument of King Ramkamhaeng, with an inscription in the Khmer language.**

Among the hill tribes, the Meo and Yao languages are related members of the Austro-Thai language family. The others are Sino-Tibetan: four Karen dialects in their own branch, and the Akha, Lahu, and Lisu tongues that are part of the Tibeto-Burman branch.

Except for the Yaos, who use Chinese characters, none of the tribal languages has its own alphabet, although missionaries have devised a way to use Roman script for many of the languages.

Sino-Thais use the older, more complex form of Chinese written characters rather than the simplified version that is favored by Chinese and Japanese people elsewhere around the world.

Thai magazines on a display rack. Numerous newspapers and magazines serve Thailand, with the provincial newspapers published once every 10 days so that they have the results of the national lottery. The most popular English newspapers are the *Bangkok Post* and *The Nation*. The *Post* has the best international news, while the *Nation* is well known for its features and opinions.

THAI AND ITS DIALECTS

The Thai language belongs to the Austro-Thai language family. Pure Thai words are single-syllabled and structured the same as Chinese. And like Chinese, it has five tones—high, low, midtone, rising, and falling.

Among the features adopted from the Khmer language were the use of prefixes and infixes, which are sound changes inserted into the word to modify the meaning. Today, it is estimated that one-third of the words used in the daily speech of Siamese Thais are of Khmer origin.

Along with adopting many Mon and Khmer words, the Thais borrowed from Sanskrit and Pali, the ancient languages of India that Buddhist monks used in their religious texts. But they altered the pronunciation to make them sound like Thai words. Inflections and accents were also dropped.

Thai and its Dialects

Besides these languages, Thai language has also taken words from English and even Malay-Javanese, thanks to the popularity of Javanese Panji tales.

Thai words are concepts by themselves and do not change according to case, number, or gender. The same word may be a noun, verb, or adjective depending on where it stands in the sentence. The basic pattern is subject-verb-object. Modifiers follow their relevant words. Articles, prepositions, and conjunctions are rare. And a Thai changes the tense or mood by adding a word.

With so many one-syllabled words, the language is filled with words that sound alike. For those with identical tones that need to be clarified, people either add words that determine their meaning or substitute words of the same meaning for them.

Thai dialects exhibit similar grammar and structure. The main differences are in vocabulary. Each of Thailand's four main regions—the north, northeast, central, and south—has its own dialect. Pak Tai, the language of the south, is close to Siamese or Central Thai, but has a strong tendency toward shortened words and fast speech. Northerners can't follow it.

By contrast, the dialects of the north and of the Isan—called Lao in the northeast—tend to lengthen sounds and syllables so that southerners and Siamese Thais have trouble understanding them. Smaller subgroups like the Shans and Thai Lue speak dialects even more different from Central Thai.

The less educated people in the regions far from Bangkok may not understand all the Central Thai they hear. But because of its tremendous media exposure—radio, TV, and movies reach everywhere—they can decipher most of it.

In the Thai language, two important words people use to express politeness are "krap" (used by men) and "ka" (used by women). One would say them after every request and reply. For example, to get somebody's attention, a man would say "kun krap" and a woman would use "kun ka."

THE THAI ALPHABET

In 1283, Sukhothai's greatest king, Ramkhamhaeng, set up a stone monument with an inscription honoring his reign. On it was a new alphabet, inspired by yet different from the Khmer alphabet, the oldest example of written Thai. Indirectly, this alphabet is based on the Tamil of South India.

In Ramkhamhaeng's inscription, both consonants and vowels are written on the same line. Eventually this system was changed so that only consonants were written on the line, vowels being written off the line. When the time came to make books, this created difficulties in setting type and locating dictionary listings, problems that persist to this day.

The Thai language has 44 consonants, plus nine vowels written in 14 different forms. Sixteen of those 44 consonants are redundant since there are 28 basic consonant sounds. There are also four tonal marks (midtone is never indicated) and 28 vowel marks. Written Thai is read from left to right, like English, and there are no spaces between words within the same sentence, a factor that certainly makes it difficult for those learning to read Thai for the first time.

MEANING IN THAI NAMES

There are tens of thousands of Thai names and every one has a meaning, although sometimes only the mother knows it. The most common are compound names with a meaning deemed good, holy, or promising. Examples: Porn (blessing), Boon (merit), Siri (glory), Som (fulfillment), Thang (gold), and Thawee (increase).

Two to three thousand names are used by both men and women. But as a general rule, boy's names are words that mean strength or honor, and

girls are named for feminine qualities—such as beauty and purity—or after flowers, plants, and fruits. However, given names are not ordinarily used. Instead, people commonly go by a nickname given early in life, either because of some obvious quality (short, tall, dark) or personality trait. Examples are *moo* (meaning pig), *noo* (mouse or rat), and *dueng* (meaning red).

Surnames are rarely used. King Rama VI introduced them as part of his own Westernization program, giving out many personally, including both Thai and Western spellings. Thais generally refer formally to one's surname only once, then switch to using the given name.

Thais like to translate their names, letter by letter, into the romanized form that we use in the West. But since most Thai names have several silent letters, the romanized versions usually bear little resemblance to the way they are actually pronounced. This applies to surnames, first names, names of streets, towns, and places. For example, King Chulalongkorn's name is pronounced "Ju-lah-long-gohrn." And if you think that's difficult, try Dasaneeyavaja. (It's pronounced "Tahsahnee-yahwed.") Sometimes the exact Thai sound just cannot be pronounced in English.

BODY LANGUAGE

Words, of course, are not the sole tools of communication among Thais. They also use a range of gestures and motions, from the obvious *wai*, to more subtle movements that make up a recognizable body language. These are used to indicate more directly what they are saying, as well as to show respect or one's place in society.

As noted earlier, the head is a sacred part of the body. Except for lovers, Thais do not touch one another's heads. Moreover, in any social encounter or gathering, the head of

During the holidays, Thais like to go to the parks in large groups and enjoy themselves by having singalong sessions.

the highest-ranking person should always be above those of everyone else. In practice this is nearly impossible to arrange, so lower-ranked people sit with their shoulders slumped or their heads lowered. When walking past a higher-ranked person, the lower-ranked person will bow his or her head in an act of recognition.

Conversely, the foot is a dishonorable part of the body. It is always taboo to point with them or display the soles to anyone. When sitting, Thais take care to keep their feet pointed behind them, in nobody's direction. Also, older or more respected people walk or sit in front of others.

The general taboo covering rowdy behavior include such normal Western traits as pointing at people, laughing in a loud unruly way, elbowing, kicking, and shouting. Thais will point with a finger at a lifeless object, but for indicating people they will use a verbal description or, if more is needed, a slight jerk of the chin in the direction of the person in question.

Thais try to keep their hands as still as possible during conversations. They do not nudge each other to get someone's attention or to make a point. Since the left hand is customarily used to clean up the body, Thais always use the right hand when passing something. If an inferior is passing something to a superior, he or she uses the left hand to support the right forearm.

THE WORLD'S LONGEST PLACE NAME

We call it Bangkok. Thais call it Krung Thep, but that's a drastic reduction. Its full name, consisting of 152 Thai letters, is: Krungthepmahanakhonbowornvatanakosinmahintaraudyamahadilokpopnoparatanarajthaniburimudomrajniwesonahasatarnamornpimarnavatarsatitsakattiyavisanukamprasit. Translated, it means "City of angels, great city of immortals, magnificent jeweled city of the god Indra, seat of the King of Ayutthaya, city of gleaming temples, city of the king's most excellent palace and dominions, home of Vishnu and all the gods." No wonder they abbreviated it!

Bangkok was not always known by this name; before it became Thailand's capital in 1782, it was just a tiny village by the Chao Phraya, and was called Bang Makok ("Bang" means riverside village and "Makok" means olive or a kind of plum).

ARTS

THE FIRST THAI efforts at storytelling were folktales told by authors whose identities have been lost in the mists of time. In the past, when not as many people could read as today, these stories were recited at the *wat* during the Buddhist Lent.

Today, this custom survives only in Nakhon Si Thammarat in the south and at Bangkok's Temple of the Emerald Buddha. But nowadays anyone can read these stories on their own.

Thailand's folk tales have their share of animal heroes, clever rogues, stupid tigers, lucky

younger brothers, monsters, and ogres. But the most popular tales are those featuring supernatural feats, romantic adventurers, and typically beautiful and helpless heroines.

The first important literature dates back to King Trailok's reign (1448–1488) when religious works like the *Phra Law* and the *Mahachat* (the Prince Vessandorn story) were composed. Classic Thai poetry formed at this time, and included a heavy dose of Sanskrit or Pali words.

Classic literature peaked just before Ayutthaya's fall. Several of King Boromakut's (1733–58) children were superb poets. Two of them composed versions of a well-known Javanese romantic poem called *Inao*, parts of which were turned into dance dramas by later generations.

LITERARY KINGS

Nearly all copies of the early Thai literary works were lost in the destruction of Ayutthaya. King Rama I, himself an accomplished poet, then called on the memories of old scholars and teachers who had survived Ayutthaya's fall and asked them to recreate such Thai classics as the *Ramakien* (an epic tale concerned with the life and adventures of Ramachandra and his wife Sita) and *Khun Chang Khun Phaen*, a Siamese love story.

Both tales provided roles for dance dramas and other performing arts. The best of the early ones were written by King Rama II—an even better poet than his father—and his contemporary, Sunthon Phu, considered Thailand's greatest classical writer. Rama II also created a dance-drama

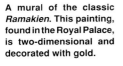

A mural of the classic *Ramakien*. This painting, found in the Royal Palace, is two-dimensional and decorated with gold.

version of *Inao*, while *Phra Abhai Mani*, an adventure through real and imaginary seas, is Sunthorn Phu's masterpiece.

Another king, Chulalongkorn, spent time recording royal ceremonies for the general reader, a valuable source for students of Thai culture. And yet another king, Vajiravudh, had a great interest in literature and was a very prolific writer. He composed poems and essays and was also the first Thai king to be educated in the West. He was a student of Shakespearean literature, and translated some of it into the Thai language. He also translated French dramas and wrote several modern plays. More than anyone else he is credited with introducing new literary forms to Thai writing. Through following generations, modern Thai literature developed. Some dealt with the past, as in Kukrit Pramoj's *Four Reigns*, while younger writers, especially Isan authors, concentrated on contemporary problems.

Dancers in a pose during a performance of the *Ramakien*. The dance is characterized by masks, heavy makeup, fancy jewelry, costumes, and headdresses that hide the face and body of each dancer.

BUDDHIST ARCHITECTURE

Within each Buddhist temple compound are several buildings and monuments. The largest, a rectangular hall with a high pointed roof, is the *bot* ("boht"), where chanting and ordinations take place. The next is the *viharn* ("vee-HARHN"), where the rituals are staged.

On a platform high off the ground stands the library, where old texts are stored. There may also be a small crematorium, recognizable by the tall chimney. The other buildings are housing for the monks.

Temple compounds contain one or more *chedi* ("CHAY–dee"). These are spire-like monuments with a broad base and a slender top that either rises like a rounded-off column or tapers to a point. The oldest of these

More than 410 feet tall, the Phra Pathom Chedi is the tallest Buddhist monument in the world. It is situated in the town of Nakhon Pathom. The original building was built more than a thousand years ago. In 1057, Burmese soldiers destroyed it. It was not until hundreds of years later that King Chulalongkorn finally rebuilt it. Situated in a square, it is surrounded by a terrace filled with trees. Every November, the building is decorated with lights and there is a big fair on the temple grounds.

are simple in design, although in some cases, such as the Wat Haripunchai in Lamphun, the entire *chedi* is plated with gold. Newer ones, such as the Wat Po in Bangkok, have ornate decorations up and down the monument.

Chedi were originally ritual objects filled with gold or silver. Such objects, however, attracted thieves and foreign armies; the destruction of ancient Ayutthaya was largely due to armies wanting to take the gold that was inside the *chedi*.

Thai art and craft benefited from the people's desire to make beautiful religious buildings. Decorations became a fine art in the temple compounds. Woodcarvers created jungle scenes on doors, window shutters, eaves, and posts. Sculptors made various sizes of Buddhas and gods in all sorts of poses. Other craftsmen fashioned chipped-glass decorations or supplied special textiles, such as the long, thin banners used in ceremonies.

Perhaps the most fascinating of all temple arts are the religious and historical murals found inside the *viharn* or *bot*. Such paintings reveal much about Thailand in centuries gone by, from clothing patterns to gods, heroes, demons, enemy soldiers, and curious European adventurers.

The graceful Bamboo
Dance of the northeast.

PERFORMING ARTS

The most fascinating new art developed under the early Chakri kings was the dance-drama, made special because it was produced by royalty and lavishly done.

There are two traditional types of dance-dramas—the *khon* ("kohn") and the *lakon* ("la–KOHN"). Originally, all *khon* performers were masked; later the in roles of gods and humans performers used crowns or headdresses, while those portraying animals and demons remain masked.

Both vocal and instrumental music, the latter played on the lute-like *phipat* ("PEE-paht"), accompany the action. There is a chorus in the cast as well. Dancers use gestures that are elegant versions of those used in daily life. The dances' stories are episodes from the *Ramakien*.

Lakon nok dramas are lively, fast-paced, with lots of rough humor. *Lakon nai* is the opposite—poetic and graceful, tender, with slow music and no vulgarity. Episodes from the *Inao* are the most common, plus other

Thai classics and tales imported from India are also performed. Scenery, now vital to the show, is a 20th century innovation.

Music and dance flourished under Vajiravudh (1910–25). But later, the world economic crisis affected royal influence and there were few shows. Responsibility for the troupes and orchestras was transferred to the government after 1934, only to be forgotten. But with the end of World War II, the government sponsored a revival, and a host of new dancers and actors were trained. Some even performed independently.

Most dances are performed by women in gorgeous costumes, with props such as candles, long attached fingernails, gossamer wings, and the crowns and headdresses of the theater. Besides those that perform for tourists, dancers are a regular feature of temple entertainment during big festivals.

Equally likely to be part of a festival program is a performance of the *likay* ("LEE-kay") theater. This is a sort of Thai version of *commedia de l'arte*, or professional group comedy. The *likay* originated in Bangkok in the 1880s. It uses both songs and dialogue, which are often vulgar, with a collection of stock characters and situations. The *likay* is usually performed without a script.

A dangerous traditional sword dance.

A young novice monk stares dreamily at the mural on the wall of a monastery.

OTHER THEATRICAL ARTS

Another kind of traditional theater replaces actors with puppets. In the south, shadow plays—similar to those of Malaysia and Indonesia—depict stories from the *Ramakien* by casting shadows from cutout leather figures onto a screen. In other places, wooden puppets—the kind familiar to the rest of the world—take the roles.

Thai Chinese have their own set of puppets, with plots from Chinese classics. They also have their traditional operas. With spectacular costumes, familiar plots and music with the emphasis on gongs and drums, Chinese operas are regularly staged in Bangkok. In coastal towns operas are sometimes presented at a private house or open park, free to all who wish to attend.

Traditional Thai orchestras accompany theater presentations. They play musical instruments like cymbals, xylophones, three-string lutes, bass fiddles, and bass drums. Large reedpipes may also be a part of the orchestra, especially in the northeast. Songs in such dramas mark the rhythm by a selected use of pitch accents instead of stressed ones, as in Western languages.

HILL TRIBAL MUSIC

Any hill tribe that has the urge to make a little music can fashion an instrument from materials in the nearest patch of jungle. Bamboo is perfect for making flutes, jew's harps, oboes, and both large and small gourd pipes.

From wood they carve the lutes and other stringed instruments plus two sizes of drums. From their buffaloes they get the hide to cover the drums, while the horns become part of the instruments. Bells and gongs complete the tribal collection of instruments.

Tribal music has its own collection of love songs and sad songs. But among hill tribes, these songs are often more than mere entertainment. Mothers pass on much of the culture through carefully worded lullabies. Other songs tell children how to behave around adults. Some that are sung during certain festivals help to reinforce cultural values.

Tribal women gather around a village musician and his pipe for a dance.

The Akhas, with their traditional village dancing ground, have perhaps the greatest body of songs in the hills. Some are in ancient Akha, and those who sing them do not even know all the words. Some are accompanied by dances. Other tribes generally dance only at big festivals, usually in groups, and often in circular patterns.

Thailand produces some of the most beautiful silk in the world, making much-loved fabrics that have been appreciated by many famous people. Among them are the United States' former first lady Eleanor Roosevelt, cosmetics queen Helena Ruben-stein, and Britain's Queen Elizabeth II. In the movie "Ben Hur" and "The King and I," Thai silk was used to make the stars' costumes. Even airlines have used this silk to decorate the interiors of their planes.

WEAVING

Thai weavers have produced some of the world's most beautiful fabrics. Most of the best are kept by the weavers themselves to be worn on special occasions, and the fanciest fabrics have, over the years, become collectors' items. Girls in the north and northeast used to be required to know how to weave in order to get married.

Thais cultivate both cotton and silk and are masters at the complex and delicate method of turning these into quality thread. Traditionally, they dyed thread with local plants—indigo particularly—or insects (lac), sometimes tying the threads into patterns before dyeing, the *ikat* process known here as *matmee* ("MUT-mee").

The typical loom is a wooden-framed handloom, with four heddles (vertical cords through which the thread is drawn), four treadles, and a bench to sit on. It can produce cloth that is about three feet wide and any length. Karens use the simpler backstrap loom, while Akhas and Meos operate a narrow, stand-up, bamboo-frame loom. Most weaving takes place in the winter—the slack time in the rural year.

JIM THOMPSON

Thailand's silk industry was dying out until it caught the eye of Jim Thompson, a former World War II American intelligence officer who was already a lover of Thai art. Directly supervising the work and introducing new color schemes, Thompson—who was called the "Father of Modern Thai Silk"—built Thai silk into a glamorous export appreciated around the world. His disappearance in 1967 during a forest walk in Malaysia is an unsolved mystery that has increased his legendary status.

EMBROIDERY

The most complex, eye-catching patterns of Thai clothing are embroidered. This can be done on the loom by adding a set of heddle sticks to lift the different warp threads in a way as to allow another weft thread to make the design. Both Thais on their big looms and Karens on their small ones do this extremely well. Northern weavers sometimes create patterns of animals and religious symbols on banners.

The other way to add embroidery is to stitch it on a finished piece, the way the Meos, Akhas, and Yaos do it. Tribal women spend much of their spare time embroidering costumes for themselves and their families. Most have a traditional range of patterns they employ, but they have been borrowing designs lately, thanks to greater contact with each other.

A worker carefully applying an overglaze decoration to stoneware, which will later be fired.

AKHA JACKETS

While chatting, feeding a baby, or even walking to the fields, an Akha woman's hands are always busy. Usually she is embroidering or applying needlework to one of her beautiful jackets.

With a zest for bold colors—the more the better—against a deep blue or black cloth, she works on patterns with names like the ordinary "riverflow," or the exotic "butterfly lips." After finishing the piece, she decorates it with things like seeds, beads, cowries, silver coins and studs, monkey fur, beetle wings, and tassels of horsetail or chicken feathers.

The wonderful gold statues of the royal palace.

SCULPTING AND PAINTING

Prior to the Sukhothai period, three main sculptural styles existed in Thailand. The oldest, by the Mon in the Dvaravati period, indicates a strong Indian influence. The next style, of the Mahayana Buddhist kingdom of Srivijaya, became popular in the eighth century. The subjects were mainly Buddhas and bodhisattvas, human-like with full Indian faces representing grace and strength.

The third, from the Khmer period, developed during the 10th century. These are realistic figures with ethnic, non-Indian faces. The sculptures are quite masculine but friendly and gentle-looking. Many of the subjects are of Hindu gods.

During the Sukhothai period, a totally new style developed. Hindu gods were still being made, but Sukhothai's contribution was to create an entirely different, very Thai representation of the Buddha, with a slender, idealized body and often a dreamy smile. Sukhothai sculptors also created a new form—the Walking Buddha, perfected in grace and elegance. Thai sculpture since Sukhothai essentially repeats and refines the forms of the original masters.

Until recently, all sculpting and painting was done for the temples or for royalty. Modern sculptors, like today's new painters, have trouble finding business as well as establishing a new style. Thai temple murals are a fascinating blend of the real with the fantastic, but modern painters rarely figure out how to move from symbolic art to more realistic, illustrative art, which depicts objects as they appear.

HANDICRAFTS

Traditionally, handicrafts were not for display but for use. All decorations were additional. Today's wealthier Thai families have the fancier things, but Thailand's antique shops are full of interesting surprises, as younger Thais with different values sell off their family antiques. If it was not for tourism, many handicraft skills would have died out years ago.

BASKETRY The traditional house needed all sorts of containers: clothing hampers, rice storage, tobacco, and betel boxes. Bamboo, rattan, teak, and rosewood were the most frequently used materials.

LACQUERWARE Elegant lacquered boxes were used to store various items. Books in the old days were long and thin; lacquered boards were sometimes used as covers, if they were not done in ivory or niello (a black metal).

PEWTER Pewter is a tin-based material used for making bowls, goblets, cups, and other objects.

JEWELRY Thais love gold and precious stones. Rubies, jade, and amber come from Myanmar but are often cut in Bangkok. Hill tribes favor chunky silver ornaments, along with jungle materials.

CERAMICS Huge water jars and smaller water pots—the latter placed in front of the house for passers-by to use—were the most common. Fired stoneware, called celadon, usually pale green in color, is the most highly-refined type.

Thailand's many wood-carvers can take a simple block of wood and make it into a masterpiece.

LEISURE

THAIS HAVE ALWAYS BEEN FOND of watching contests of strength and skill. In earlier days, the most impressive display was the ancient Mon sport of swordfighting. Opponents held two swords and fought with eye-blurring precision. A similar combat was also staged with sticks.

Nowadays the more popular entertainment is Thai kickboxing. This is different from ordinary boxing in that fighters also use their feet, using various types of kicks and punches.

Thai kickboxing originated during the Ayutthaya period, when it was a self-defense technique. Later it was adapted into today's spectator sport. Kickboxing champions usually become popular heroes.

Thailand regularly produces world champion boxers, usually in the lighter weight divisions of the World Boxing Association. Thai boxing fans also like to follow the fortunes of Western heavyweights and other famous boxers. Any internationally televised championship fight is likely to interrupt all work while the men gather round to cheer on their favorites.

Next to kickboxing and boxing, soccer is the most popular competitive sport. School games are heavily supported and the fortunes of the national team in international matches are closely followed.

Above: **A fighter delivers a kick at his opponent in Thailand's dangerous but popular sport of kick-boxing.**

Opposite: **Sunday morning at one of Bangkok's numerous parks finds a young girl practicing her keyboard by a pond.**

99

ANIMAL COMBATS

Cockfighting is taken very seriously by many Thais, for whom it is a favorite pastime, especially after the January rice harvest. Owners raise such cocks separately from other chickens. From when they are eight months old, these birds are mixed with adult cocks and trained for deadly combat.

Fights are usually held in small circular stadiums. The cocks are blindfolded and their spurs not armed until the fight is ready to begin. Heavy gambling accompanies each round, along with the cheering and loud shouting that follows winning and losing.

Near these same arenas, there are often small aquariums containing fish the size of a child's finger. These are the famous Thai fighting fish that nudge and push each other. Spectators gather to place their bets on which fish will win the fight, while at the same time cheering for their favorites.

In the hillside villages, children go around looking for armored beetles. They capture these beetles and tie them onto a stick. By prodding them with a straw, they induce the insects to lock horns and wrestle.

GAMES

Board games of various kinds were popular in the past. Others were played with sticks and cowries, which are tablets with numbers or Chinese characters inscribed on them that look like dominoes. Thai chess resembles the Chinese kind; there are 64 squares as in Western chess, but with different moves.

Among Thai royalty, checkers and polo are favorite games, along with one called *rua pung* ("ROO-a POONG"). The game is played on a field 132 feet long and only three and a half feet wide, enclosed by banana trees,

and filled with sand or rice paddy husk. The object is to see who can hurl the *rua pung* shot the farthest and straightest downfield.

Gambling with dice, cards, or other things has always been a common pastime. These games provide players with good company and cheap entertainment, no matter what happens to their money.

Thai children also have their own games. In one, known as the "ee-tak" or scoop game, they try to pick up fruit seeds one at a time from a pile using a special paper scoop without disturbing the other seeds. Another is the "snake eats its tail," where two of the strongest children play the father and mother snakes. The rest play baby snakes and form a chain behind the mother snake. The object is for the "mother" to prevent the "father" from catching the "babies."

An enthusiastic crowd gathers around a cock-fighting stadium to cheer on their favorites.

EXERCISE

More and more city dwellers are becoming interested in physical exercise. Early each morning, Bangkok's large Lumphini Park becomes crowded with office workers and other professionals jogging, doing *taiji* ("tai-chee"), gymnastics, or some form of exercise. Even the provincial towns have parks that are filled with joggers every morning or evening.

The simplest, most popular exercise in which people can participate in is *takraw* ("TAH-krohr"). Players gather in a wide circle and kick or head a ball made of strips of rattan, the only object being to keep it from hitting the ground. An improvement to this simple game was the addition of a high basket during the 1930s. The object then is to send it through the basket, with points scored according to the difficulty of the shot.

A jogger huffs and puffs his way through his morning run in one of Thailand's many jogging parks.

Teams compete on either side of a net in *sepak takraw* ("SAY-pahk TAH-krohr"). The rules and scoring are like those in volleyball, except players can only use their feet, and they are allowed to freely change positions.

Thais love betting on sports and games, which even accompanies the annual kite fights. These kites are pentagonal and star-shaped, without tails. An unusual jerk of the string is enough to send the kite flying. "Male" kites try to capture "female" kites by entangling and sawing the strings off.

RECREATION

The Thai word for fun is *sanuk* ("sah-NOOK"), and a good sense of *sanuk* is supposed to fill the atmosphere of both work and play. Interpreting the word more broadly, it means having a cheerful, carefree attitude toward the entertainment and games at any social gathering. Being a friendly and sociable people, Thais always go out in groups, or seldom alone, and the company is usually every bit as much *sanuk* as the event itself.

Thais have a great variety of leisure options. There are golf courses and nature parks throughout the country, snooker (a game similar to pool) halls in every town (there are 800 in Bangkok alone), city parks for picnics, and spas for those pursuing better health. There is a wide range of entertainment possibilities as well as an incredible number of travel agencies offering domestic or international tour packages.

Islands and beaches are well used, especially on weekends when student and office groups head for them. Boating, windsurfing, snorkeling, diving, and parasailing are among the major attractions there.

Strictly no hands: that is the Thai form of volleyball called *sepak takraw*. It is as common to Thai boys as baseball is to Americans. This game dates back hundreds of years to the reign of King Rama II.

ENTERTAINMENT

In earlier times, when monks used to spend their spare time solving difficult or complicated mathematical puzzles, the ordinary people instead flocked to watch special marionette shows, theater presentations, or performances by acrobats on 20-foot high poles.

People amuse themselves differently nowadays. Most city people have a television and almost everyone has a radio. While video games have lost their popularity, video tapes are currently the rage. There are over 7,000 video rental shops in Bangkok alone, and video halls (places where the public can go and watch videos) have invaded the peace and quiet of even remote hill villages.

One night in Bangkok: the dance clubs and lounges are filled every night with young Thais, who bop to the latest hits from around the world. One of the most fascinating discos in town is called the NASA; it has a real space capsule to go along with its special laser effects and extremely loud music.

Thai movies have yet to win international acclaim because their plots are generally mundane and predictable, with stereotypical characters. Martial arts movies—especially Hong Kong productions dubbed in Thai— and love triangle sagas seem to be the most popular.

Night life in the city is quite active. Most discos, bars, and lounges stay open past midnight, as do restaurants. A typical Thai cocktail lounge will have a female singer with a backup band playing—not much different from lounges in the West.

Shopping malls, night markets, and streetside dining places are also entertainment spots for Thais; people watching and "window shopping" are some of the ways they entertain themselves.

Lunch time and *sanuk* in one of Bangkok's many hotels.

FESTIVALS

AS IS FITTING FOR A MONARCHY, the birthdays of the king and queen of Thailand are important national holidays. Schools and government offices are carefully decorated and the area around the grand palace in Bangkok is lit up spectacularly, accompanied by fireworks.

Below: **Watch out! Thai youths having fun during the Songkran festival, when everybody gets drenched in water.**

With less pomp, Thais also honor Chakri Day—the founding day of the current dynasty—and Coronation Day, which marks the rise of King Bhumibol to the crown.

King Chulalongkorn's achievements are acknowledged another day when people lay wreaths before his statue. Two days before the king's birthday, the colorful Royal Guards troop by the Royal Family to renew their oath of loyalty.

Below: **Watch out! Thai youths having fun during the Songkran festival, when everybody gets drenched in water.**

Previously, the king personally took part in the royal ploughing ceremony, a rite staged every April to announce the start of the planting season. But since the reign of King Mongkut, the king only attends the event while his delegate, usually the minister of agriculture, ploughs three symbolic troughs. Later, several prophecies are read and interpreted in various ways to the king.

Opposite: **On *Loy Krathong*, thousands of tiny candlelit boats (like this one) shaped like lotuses are set on every pond or waterway. This takes place on the night of the full moon of the 12th lunar month; the exact date varies every year.**

Loy Krathong is from the legend of a beautiful and talented woman named Kang Noppamas, who made the first krathong 700 years ago. Honoring Mother Water in her own way, she made the krathong and presented it to King Ramkham-haeng, who accepted it, lit the candle in it, and launched it on water.

Opposite: Festival floats during the popular Loy Krathong, which is Hindu in origin. On this occasion people rejoice in the Mother Water's gifts to them. To some, it is a chance to ask the water spirits for forgiveness for polluting their water and to take away their bad luck. To others, it is just a joyful occasion.

TRADITIONAL THAI FESTIVALS

NATIONWIDE As a Buddhist country, Thailand celebrates important anniversaries with ceremonies that give Buddhists around the country an opportunity to do their part in merit-making, with gifts to monks and candlelit processions at night. Sometimes there are also gatherings where religious tales are told.

Magha Puja in February marks the day 1,250 disciples assembled to hear the Buddha preach. And the Visakha Puja in May celebrates the birth, enlightenment, and death of the Buddha.

The *Khao Phansa*, in July, announces the start of the Buddhist Lent—which is the annual monsoon retreat. It ends three months later with the period of Kathin, when the people give monks new robes.

In the traditional calendar, New Year comes on April 13. But the Thai New Year, better known as *Songkran*, is an occasion not only for merit-making, but also for enjoyment. This is the occasion when people go around dousing one another with water from cups, buckets, or hoses.

The most beautiful event of the year is the *Loy Krathong*, held for three days during the full moon of November. *Krathong* are small candles or lamps mounted on floats made from leaves. During the night, every stretch of water in Thailand will be filled with thousands of candles inside beautiful little leaf baskets. In Chiang Mai, the tradition includes the release of giant hot-air balloons. Everywhere, processions, fireworks, and lights grace these three nights.

REGIONAL While everyone participates in the national festivals many provinces have unique events of their own. Among the most interesting are:

Lampang's Luang Wiang Lakon during February—a stately procession of Buddhist images that includes participation by the former royal family of Chiang Mai.

Yasothon's Rocket Festival in the northeast—the firing of homemade rockets of all sizes, which the people believe will ensure a good monsoon and abundant harvests.

Loei's Phi Ta Khon in June—a merry re-enactment of spirits celebrating Prince Vessandorn's return to his city, as people dress up as ghosts for the day.

Phichit's Boat Races in September—an annual event on the Nan River in low-slung wooden boats.

Surat Thani's Chak Phra in October—Buddha images mounted on carriages are hauled through the streets and floated on rivers and canals.

Chonburi's Buffalo Races in October—the parading and racing of the Thai farmer's most valuable animal.

Sakhon Nakhon's Wax Castle Festival in October—the making of beautiful miniature temples in beeswax.

Nan's Lanna Boat Races in October—the giving of robes to local monks, accompanied by races in brightly-painted wooden boats.

A lion dance takes place in Bangkok during the Chinese New Year celebrations. For Thailand's few million Chinese, this is the occasion for family reunions, huge feasts, gift giving, and a chance to close up businesses for a few days.

CHINESE FESTIVALS

Thailand's Chinese population celebrates the Lunar New Year in late January or early February. Merchants take a rest, offices close for several days, and all sorts of decorations go up. Loud noise is the hallmark of the celebration, along with the burning of paper notes, fireworks, and processions.

Large Chinese communities around the country also stage lion and dragon dances. The most spectacular displays are held at Nakhon Sawan, where the Chinese honor the Golden Dragon with a grand parade.

In the south during the last century, Chinese immigrants in Phuket and Trang started an unusual annual Vegetarian Festival that has become the event of the year in these cities.

During this celebration, the Chinese go on a 10-day vegetarian diet and stage many parades, also performing such strange feats as walking across a bed of burning coals and piercing their faces with sharp steel rods. They are said to be in a trance during these performances, and they show no signs of pain.

OTHER FESTIVALS

MOSLEM Ramadan is the most important event in the Islamic calendar. Moslems fast 12 to 15 hours a day for one month while attending mosques for religious studies in the evenings. A great feast, called Id al Fitr, marks the end of the period. They also observe Hijra Day, which commemorates the Prophet Mohammed's trip to the city of Medina (also the first day of the Islamic year). Moslems also observe the Haj, the traditional annual pilgrimage to Mecca.

MON The Mons of Samut Prakan, south of Bangkok, celebrate their own Songkran with a thorough housecleaning, various rites, and processions.

SHAN Shans are a majority in Mae Hong Son, where in April they hold the Poy Sanglong ceremony. Young novices about to enter monkhood are dressed in beautiful costumes and carried through the towns.

The never-ending pursuit of "sanuk" guarantees Thais endless festivals. The greatest number of festivals occur during the cool part of the year, from November to February. The dates are not always the same each year because they are determined by the Thai lunar calendar, which is a few days shorter than the solar calendar.

THE GIANT SWING

In downtown Bangkok stands a wooden frame, 60 feet high, to which a swing was once annually attached for the most dangerous rite of Thailand's numerous festivals. To invite the Indian gods Phra Ruan (Shiva) and Phra Narai (Vishnu) to visit the Earth, a young Indian with two assistants rode the giant swing to seize, on the arc, a money bag with his teeth. The three men risked life and limb to collect a bag that only contained eight to 12 baht.

A unique and time-honored rite, the giant swing ride was discontinued in 1935 because the support beams were no longer strong enough to hold the men.

An Akha couple on a swing during a tribal festival. The Akhas build these swings and hold swing-ride ceremonies for the Women's New Year in the latter part of the rainy season.

TRIBAL FESTIVALS

All hill tribes celebrate New Year, though not on the same day. Karens, Lisus, Yaos, and some Lahus observe it the same day as the Chinese, and most Yao rites closely resemble Chinese practices. Other Lahus, Akhas, and Meos hold their New Year a month or so earlier. The slaughtering of animals, rounds of heavy feasting and drinking, and lots of singing and dancing characterize the event.

Among the hill people, the New Year is also the beginning of the courting season, so young men and women dress up to show off. Meo youths line up opposite one another and toss balls back and forth—a perfect chance to introduce oneself. Adolescent Akhas beat bamboo drums together throughout the night. And Lisus dance in small groups around the village priest's tree to the music of gourd pipes and lutes.

Only at this time of year do young boys spin tops and try to knock each others' out by hurling theirs against their opponents' standing tops. In Akha villages, women go for a ride on a big swing that is not allowed to be used the rest of the year.

Tribes stage ceremonies to start the rice-planting season, to bless the autumn harvest and to please guardian spirits or the invisible "lords of the land" they consider the real owners of their rice fields. Among the Karens, there is also a yearly ritual to please the spirit of their ancestors, presided over by the oldest woman. Meos hold one for the door spirit and another for the spirit of the central house post. Every year, Yaos beg for forgiveness from the mountain spirit for allowing their animals to graze freely on its turf.

Bad spirits must be kept out of the village area. So each September, Akha boys make wooden swords to chase them out, dashing through each house in the village. Lisus people trick the spirits into going to a feast outside the line of defensive taboo signs that marks the village boundary, through which spirits cannot pass.

Festivals allow or even require people to do things they otherwise would not do at other times of the year. Rules commanding a communal feast, for instance, assure every family of a portion of protein-rich meat. But other festival rules simply guarantee fun.

Something new: the true "cow" boys—the annual Chonburi Buffalo Races.

In full make-up and fake mustaches, Ubon children in costume have some fun during a performance.

MAKING NEW FESTIVALS

With their love for *sanuk*, Thais are constantly inventing new "excuses" for festivals. Civic groups and business organizations support them. The usual program includes displays, exhibits, entertainment of various sorts, processions, maybe a float parade, and definitely a beauty contest.

The most famous of these new festivals, started in 1960, is the Elephant Round-up in Surin in the northeast. This is an authentic re-enactment of how wild elephants were captured and trained in the past. Both working and war elephants are used during the event.

The Tourism Authority of Thailand always plays a key role in promoting the various local product fairs. Among them are festivals for the umbrellas of Bor Sang, the flowers of Chiang Mai, the straw birds of Chainat, and the silk of Khon Kaen. Fruit fairs are featured at Rayong, Trat, Chanthaburi, and Nakhon Pathom, while specific fairs are held for the mango at Chachoengsao, the grape at Ratchaburi, the lychee at Chiang Rai, the rambutan at Surat Thani, the longan at Lamphun, the banana at Kamphaeng Phet, the *langsat* at Uttaradit, and the custard apple at Nakhon Ratchasima!

OFFICIAL THAI HOLIDAYS

New Year's Day	January 1
Magha Puja	February
Chakri Day	April 6
Songkran	April 13
Visakha Puja	May
Royal Ploughing Ceremony	May
Khao Phansa	July
Queen's Birthday	August 12
Chulalongkorn Day	October 23
Loy Krathong	November
King's Birthday	December 5
Constitution Day	December 10
New Year's Eve	December 31

BEAUTY CONTESTS

Thais love beauty contests; they are always treated with the atmosphere of a festival. And with good reason; Thai women are famous for their breathtaking beauty. Winners of major pageants always make the front-page news and become instant celebrities.

In 1965, when Apasara Hongsakul was crowned Miss Universe, the country erupted into celebration. Her crowning revealed to much of the world, for the first time, the beauty of Thai women. Two decades later, Thailand again went wild when Porntip Narkhirunkanok was crowned Miss Universe 1988. She was called a "national heroine." Even the government congratulated her and assigned her diplomatic duties.

Every festival in Thailand has its beauty contest or two. Every year, including the national pageant with its provincial semifinals, someone is chosen Miss Thailand, Miss Thailand World, Mrs. Thailand, Miss Hill Tribe, Miss Farmer's Daughter, Miss Umbrella, Miss Mango, Miss Grape, Miss Longan, Miss Banana, Miss Lychee, and—in an extreme case—even Miss Transvestite.

The Red Cross Fair, held every January or February, is opened by Queen Sirikit, the Thai Red Cross's honorary president. The fair is filled with stalls operated by foreign embassies, Thai movie stars, various universities, and government departments. There is also classical and folk dancing as well as other entertainment. The money made at the fair is then donated to the Red Cross.

FOOD

THAI FOOD COMBINES Chinese and Indian influences with its own native recipes. Most famous are the curries and the spicy hot seasoned stews, plus the smooth and tasty coconut curries.

Most meals use rice as the filler, but there are many noodle dishes and salads without rice. Ovens are not part of the ordinary Thai kitchen or small restaurant, for cooked food is either boiled, fried, or stir-fried.

Thai food is never bland. Its range of spices includes chili, pepper, coriander leaf and root, lemon grass, basil, ginger, mint, cardamom, and screwpine. Sour soups are popular and meat and fish are always served with sauces like shrimp paste, tamarind, or honey with chili. Fish sauce is the basic substitute for salt across the country.

Spicy salads are a local specialty. They are made from raw prawns, meat, green papaya, field crab, or chopped raw meat, with a lot of chili and other spices. Like the various noodle dishes, they are often sold at streetside stalls for those who want a light meal.

Thais have no food bias and are always willing to try any sort of meat, wild or domestic, and most seafood. It is not unusual to see a menu with dishes like frog, snake, lizard, and deer offered.

Thais like to eat whenever they are in the mood, at any hour of the day or night. Their motto has always been: "Eat when you are hungry."

A TRADITIONAL MEAL

Before Western influence introduced tables and chairs, Thais dined by sitting on the floor around a small, short table. Various curries and other dishes were set upon the table, like cabbage and greenbean, skewered or fried meat, crab or fish. The hot, sour soup that is part of any full-course Thai meal was cooked in a clay pot that was placed in the center of the table.

Rice was served in small bowls to each person, who then used spoons or chopsticks to select pieces of food from the other bowls. Each diner also had a separate soup bowl that he or she filled from the common pot.

That ancient style of eating has not changed much; the only exception is that the food has been transferred to a taller table. Soup is still cooked in the center, if not in a clay pot then in a wheel-shaped pan. But throughout the countryside, the old way still exists.

RICE

Several months of hard labor go into providing Thai supper tables with their most important food—rice. Farmers have to break up the hard ground during the dry season of the year and plough it with the first drops

of rain. Rice seedlings are first planted in one part of the field, where they grow while the farmer cultivates and prepares another part of the field in which the rice will be transplanted at the start of the heavy rain season.

Weeds and pests attack the rice fields all summer. Hoppers, rice bugs, field crabs, mice, and herons keep the farmers busy. After the rains comes the harvest, followed by the exhausting job of threshing, winnowing, and milling the rice grains.

Most Thais prefer the highly-polished variety called *khao suai*, or "beautiful rice." The people of Isan eat mainly sticky rice—*khao nio*. Northern hill tribes grow a different variety that requires no transplanting, and which they mill only just before cooking. It is less polished and called *khao doi*, or "mountain rice."

Sweets galore! In Thailand, you can eat exotic stuff like sticky rice baked in bamboo, banana fritters, mango and sticky rice with coconut sauce and fruit, beans or jelly with sweet juice, and shaved ice.

119

PLA NAM—FISH IN RED SAUCE

1½ lb fish fillet
4 tbsp oil
2 onions, finely chopped
4 ripe tomatoes, peeled and chopped
2 tbsp of vinegar
salt and pepper
2–3 fresh chili peppers, seeded and chopped
3–4 tbsp chopped fresh cilantro

Heat oil and fry onions over medium heat until soft and golden brown. Add tomatoes, vinegar, salt and pepper to taste, and chili peppers. Cover and simmer for 20 minutes or until tomatoes are pulpy and sauce thick. Add fish, cover and cook until fish is done. Serve hot, sprinkled with chopped cilanto. Serves 4–6.

REGIONAL TASTES

ISAN While Thais of the Central Plains eat glutinous rice with sweets, the northeasterners of the Isan serve steamed sticky rice as the main filler for a meal, where it is taken by the handful and rolled into a ball. Isan dishes include parts of animals you would not ordinarily think of as edible, like lungs and cows' lips.

There are three sauces that accompany these meals: one bitter, one thick and spicy hot, and one thin with chilies.

LANNA The people of this northern region frequently take sticky rice as the main filler. They like bamboo shoots in their dishes, with spiced raw beef, ox giblets, fermented ground pork, and special Chiang Mai sausages. *Kao soi*, a Chiang Mai noodle curry, is a favorite snack.

THE SOUTH Sour curries with melon or morning glory are popular with the people of the Malay Peninsula, along with fried sator seed, rice noodle curry, skewered meat with peanut sauce (satay), and—with sea on either side of the peninsula—all types of seafood, from shark steaks to cockles and mussels.

TRIBAL FOOD

Like traditional Thais, tribal people sit around a low square or round table that is loaded with various dishes of curries, meat and vegetables. Tables and bowls, plates and cups are all fashioned from bamboo and rattan. Chopsticks and spoons complete the utensils. A bit of alcohol, made from distilled rice, might come with the meal, especially during ceremonies.

Hill tribes eat practically anything. Besides what they raise for themselves on their farms, they gather a great variety of edible plants, roots, brackens, and fruits from the jungles near their villages. In certain seasons, they even gather insects like bamboo grubs and wild bee larvae, which they consider good to eat.

Spring is the best hunting season, when the fields are burned to drive the animals out of the bushes. With snare traps, long-barreled homemade rifles or even crossbows, hunters search for rabbits, barking deer, civets, monitor lizards, squirrels, and even wild boars or bears. Even when working in the fields, they set traps to catch small birds, which they toss into a fire to both burn off the feathers and cook the meat.

When tribes have a feast, the animal they use as a sacrifice could be a pig (during weddings, for example), a buffalo (funerals), a chicken (spirit or ancestor worship) or even a dog (only in the Akha tribes). The meat is usually divided equally among clan or village households.

Hill tribe people using a traditional method to work or clean their rice. Despite the passing of time and contact with the rest of the world, rice is still the number one food among Thais.

Andaman Sea   A3
Ayutthaya   B3

Bangkok   B3

CaoNguyen Khorat   B2
Chao Phraya, river   B2
Chanthaburi   B3
Chi, river   C2
Chiang Mai   A1
Chon Buri   B3

Gulf of Thailand   B4
Gulf of Tonkin   D1

Hat Yai   B5

Kampuchea   C3
Kho Khot Kra   A4

Lampang   A1
Lam Pao reservoir   C2
Laos   C1

Malay Peninsula   A5
Mekong, river   B1
Mukdahan   C2
Mun, river   B2
Myanmar   A1

Nakhon Pathorn   B3
Nakhon Ratchasima   B2
Nakhon Sawan   B2
Nakhon Si Thammarat   B5
Nan   B1

Pattani   B5
Phattaya   B3
Phet Buri   A3
Phitsanulok   B2
Phuket   A5
Ping, river   A2

Samut Songkhram   B3
Songkhla   B5
South China Sea   D4
Surat Thani   A4

Thale Luang   B5
Thon Buri   B3

Ubon Ratchathani   C2
Udon Thani   B2

Vietnam   D3

Yom, river   B2

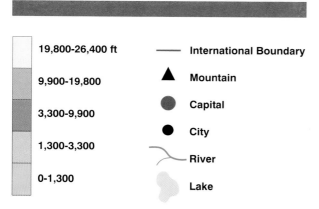

19,800-26,400 ft

9,900-19,800

3,300-9,900

1,300-3,300

0-1,300

—— International Boundary

▲ Mountain

● Capital

● City

River

Lake

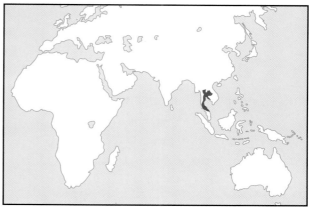

QUICK NOTES

AREA
198,456 square miles

POPULATION
56.8 million

CAPITAL
Bangkok

PROVINCES
Ang Thong, Ayutthaya, Bangkok, Buriram, Chachoengsao, Chainat, Chaiyaphum, Chanthaburi, Chiang Mai, Chiang Rai, Chon Buri, Chumphon, Kalasin, Kamphaeng Phet, Kanchanaburi, Khon Kaen, Krabi, Lampang, Lamphun, Loei, Lop Buri, Mae Hong Son, Maha Sarakham, Mukdahan, Nakhon Nayok, Nakhon Pathom, Nakhon Phanom, Nakhon Ratchasima, Nakhon Sawan, Nakhon Si Thammarat, Nan, Narathiwat, Nonthaburi, Nong Khai, Pathum Thani, Pattani, Petchabun, Phangnga, Phatthalung, Phayao, Phetchabun, Phichit, Phitsanulok, Phrae, Phuket, Prachin Buri, Prachuap Khirikhan, Ranong, Rat Buri, Rayong, Roi Et, Sakon Nakhon, Samut Prakan, Samut Sakhon, Samut Songkhram, Sara Buri, Satun, Sing Buri, Sisaket, Songkhla, Sukhothai, Suphan Buri, Surat Thani, Surin, Tak, Trang, Trat, Ubon Ratchathani, Udon Thani, Uthai Thani, Uttaradit, Yala, Yasothon.

HIGHEST POINT
Doi Inthanon, Chiang Mai Province, 8,514 feet

MAJOR RELIGION
Buddhism

OFFICIAL LANGUAGE
Thai

CURRENCY
Baht ($1 = 25–26 baht)

MAIN EXPORTS
Rice, rubber, tin, seafood, textiles, clothing.

IMPORTANT ANNIVERSARIES
June 24—marks the day in 1932 when the Thais overthrew absolute monarchy, and created a constitutional monarchy.
October 14—day in 1973 when thousands of students marched in Bangkok to force the military dictatorship to resign.

GREAT THAI KINGS
Ramkhamhaeng—famous Sukhothai king.
Rama I—founder of current Chakri dynasty.
Mongkut—made contact with the West.
Chulalongkorn—regarded as the greatest king.
Bhumibol Adulyadej—the current king.

GLOSSARY

bot	("boht") The largest building in a temple compound, used for prayer and ordination.
chedi	("CHAY-dee") Spire-like devotional monument.
khao	("kao") Cooked rice.
khon	("kohn") Traditional masked dance drama.
khwan	("kwahn") Soul, or life-force.
klong	("klohng") Canal.
krathong	("kra-TOHNG") Floating devotional lamp.
krengjai	("KRENG-jai") Consideration of those one must respect.
likay	("LEE-kay") Improvisational theater.
matmee	("MUT-mee") Technique of resist-dyeing to produce desired patterns.
mai noi	("mee-a-NOI") Additional, "minor" wife.
muban	("MOO-bahn") Village.
pha sin	("PAH SIN") Traditional Thai woman's wraparound sarong.
phi	("pee") Spirits.
phipat	("PEE-paht") Lute-like stringed instrument.
sanuk	("sah-NOOK") Amusement, enjoyment.
tambon	("TAHM-bohn") Administrative unit of 10–15 villages.
viharn	Temple compound building used for rituals.
wai	("wai") Traditional folded hands greeting.
wat	A temple compound.

BIBLIOGRAPHY

Bendel, Ruth Thompson: *Bangkok, A Thai Diary*, Asia Pacific Press, Singapore, 1972.

Cooper, Robert and Nanthapa: *Culture Shock! Thailand,* Times Editions, Singapore, 1990.

Goldfarb, Mace: *Fighters, Refugees, Immigrants: A Story of the Hmong*, Lerner, Minneapolis, 1982.

Hoskin, John: *Bangkok,* Times Editions, Singapore, 1990.

Landon, Margaret: *Anna and the King of Siam*, Harper and Row, New York, 1944.

McNair, Sylvia: *Thailand*, Children's Press, Chicago, 1987.

Orihara, Kei: *Children of the World: Thailand*, Gareth Stevens, Milwaukee, 1988.

Segaller, Dennis: *Thai Ways,* Post Publishing, Bangkok, 1985.

Segaller, Dennis: *More Thai Ways*, Allied Newspapers, Bangkok, 1982.

Wilkins, Frances: *Let's Visit Thailand*, Burke Publishing Co., Bridgeport, Conn., 1985.

Wilkins, Frances: *Thailand*, Chelsea House, New York, 1988.

INDEX

agriculture 35, 37, 46, 119
Akhas 31, 47, 59, 61, 77, 93, 95, 112
alphabet 21, 80
amulets 74
Andaman Sea 7, 14
animism 70
army 33, 61
Ayutthaya 10, 19, 21, 22, 24, 42, 67, 83, 86, 89

Ban Chiang 19
Bangkok 7, 10, 11, 24, 27, 35, 36, 39, 44, 51, 60, 83, 91, 102, 103, 104, 105, 107, 110
Bhumibol, Adulyadej (Rama IX) 27, 107
Bilauktaung Range 14
Boromakot, King 23
Boromaraja II, King 22
boxing 99

Britain 24
British East India Company 23
Buddhism 43, 52, 59, 62, 67-69, 70, 74, 88, 108
Burma (Myanmar) 7, 13, 22, 23, 33, 42, 46, 75

Cabinet of 14 Ministers 29
Chakri Dynasty 24, 107
Chantaburi 10
Chao Phraya Chakri (see Rama I)
Chao Phraya River 10, 12, 83
Chiang Mai 10, 12, 22, 32, 42, 74, 108, 114
Chiang Rai 12
Chiang Saen 12
China 13, 42,
Chinese 43, 48, 54, 62, 67, 70, 77, 92, 110
Chinese New Year 110
Chonburi Buffalo Races 113

INDEX

Christianity 23, 67, 71
Chuan Leekpai 27
Chulalongkorn 24, 30, 68, 81, 87, 88, 107
Chulalongkorn and Thammasat universities 60
climate 7, 44
cockfighting 100
Communists 26, 33

Dutch 23
Dvaravati kingdom 20

education 57, 60
elephants 39
Europeans 23

Floating Markets 11, 42
Four Reigns (by Kukrit Pramoj) 87
France, French 23, 24, 25

Golden Triangle 13, 46
Great Depression 25
Guizhou Province, China 41, 43
Gulf of Thailand 8, 14

Hat Yai 14
hill tribes 31, 46, 55, 93, 112, 121
Himalaya Mountains 8, 12
headman 31
Hong Kong 36, 105
Htins 49

Inao 85, 86, 91
India, Indians 8, 54, 73, 78, 80, 91
Isan 13, 44, 79, 87, 120

jai yen, jai rohn 51, 53
Japan, Japanese 17, 26, 35, 73

Kampuchea 7, 26, 42, 49
Kanchanaburi 10, 17, 19
Karens 43, 48, 59, 77, 94, 95, 112
Khamus 49
Khmers 18, 20, 21, 42, 44, 67, 75, 77, 78, 80
Khun Chang Khun Phaen 86

khwan 68
kickboxing 99
Ko Kian 19
Ko Phi Phi Island 7
krengjai 51, 53
Kwai Yai River, bridge 17

Lahus 48, 112
Lanna (people) 120
Laos (country) 7, 26, 46, 49
Laos (tribe) 13, 44
Lawas 49
Lop Buri 10
likay theater 91
Lisus 48, 59, 77, 112
Lop Buri 20
lotus flower 15, 107
Louis XIV 23

Malay Peninsula 8, 14, 20, 21, 120
Malays 43
Malaysia 7, 42, 92
Mae Sa waterfalls 8
meditation 73
Meklang, river 17
Mekong, river 13, 20, 117
Mae Nam Chao Phraya Basin 10, 14, 20
Meos 48, 59, 77, 94, 95, 112
military training 57
Mlabris 49
Mongkut 24, 35, 68, 71, 107
monks 54, 69
Mons 20, 21, 42, 67, 77, 78, 99, 111
Moslems 33, 43, 63, 71, 111
muban 30

Nakhon Pathom 10, 20, 88, 114
Nakhon Pathom Chedi 88
Nakhon Si Thammarat 14, 20, 21, 85
Nan, river 12
Napoleonic Wars 24
Narai 23
Naresuan 23
Nok Tha 19

INDEX

official holidays 115

pai tio 61
Pak Tai 79
pakama (Thai headpiece) 52
parliament 28, 29
Pasak, river 12
Pattani 14, 23
pha sin 45
Phaulkon, Constantine 23
Phayao 12
phi 56, 67
Pibun Songgram 26
Phimai 20
Phnom Penh 22
Phra Abbai Mani 86
Phuket 14
Ping, river 12
Prem Tinsulananda 27

Rama I 24, 25
Rama II 39, 86
Rama VI 25, 81, 87
Rama VII 25
Rama VIII 26
Ramakien 67, 86, 87, 90, 92
Ramkhamhaeng 21, 77, 80
Ranong 14
refugees 49
reptiles 16
Revolution of 1932 25, 33

Sakai 42
sanuk 100, 102, 103, 105, 111, 114
school, college 56, 60
sepak takraw 103
Shan 79, 111
silk 94
slash-and-burn 37, 46
slavery 22
soccer 99
socialism 26, 27
Songkhla 14
Songkran festival 48, 107, 108

Sukhothai 7, 20, 21, 22, 67, 96

Tai 41
takraw 102
Taowetsuwan 56
tattoos 75
Thai massage 73
Theravada Buddhism 68, 70
Thompson, Jim 94
Tilokaraja, King 22
Trailok, King 22

United States 24, 25, 26, 27, 35

Vajiravudh, King 87, 91
Vessandorn 71, 85
Vietnam 26, 27, 49

Wang, river 12
wai 52, 54, 62, 82
wat 70, 85
Wat Raj Burana 19
Women's New Year 112
World War II 9, 17, 33, 43, 91

Yaos 48, 59, 77, 95, 112
Yom, river 12
Yunnan Province, China 41, 43

PICTURE CREDITS
APA: 3
Jim Goodman: 15, 16, 18, 32, 35, 37, 45, 47, 53, 57, 68, 71, 73, 77, 78, 93, 95, 98, 109, 113, 118
Life File Photo Library: 10, 17, 29, 55, 66, 67, 91, 114, 121, 123
George Mann: 9, 12, 31, 36, 48, 49, 51, 58, 60, 72, 82, 85, 90, 99, 102, 104, 107, 112, 119
Dominic Sansoni: 4, 5, 54, 69, 92, 116
Bernard Sonneville: 1, 7, 11, 19, 21, 22, 30, 38, 39, 41, 42, 46, 63, 70, 74, 81, 86, 87, 88, 89, 96, 105, 110, 117
Luca Invernizzi Tettoni: 6, 8, 14, 25, 27, 28, 33, 34, 40, 44, 50, 65, 76, 83, 84, 97, 101, 103, 106, 120